Look UP
Look IN
Look OUT

3 Simple Steps to a
Divinely Guided Life

LISA TAYLOR

Hardcover ISBN: 978-1-960876-99-7
Paperback ISBN: 978-1-967703-00-5
Ebook ISBN: 978-1-967703-10-4
Library of Congress Control Number: 2025937735

Muse Literary Publishing

Send feedback to hello@museliterary.com
Special discounts for bulk sales are available, please contact operations@museliterary.com

This book is dedicated to you . . .

You, Who Listen to the Still Small Voice
Who Follow with a Humble Heart
Who Dare to Live as Soul Expressed,
Guided and Empowered by Omnipotence
You, Who Claim True Selfhood, Give All, and Serve

and

To Bunnynose and the *woman in the cave.*

Contents

Introduction

I was hot-dogging my way down a mogul field and stupidly stopped just below a bump to look up the slope for my dad. In that quick glance, what I saw was not my dad, but a guy, much older and larger than I was, coming right at me, out of control, and yelling something incomprehensible. He came flying off the mogul, skis first, right into me, and we both went down in a flurry of snow and skis and poles. Scraping to a stop, I quickly realized that my ten-year-old shin — having abruptly stopped his hurtling body — had lost the battle with his skis.

This is not how I imagined our first day on the slopes. My dad had invited me on this ski weekend in Vermont a year after my parents divorced. The youngest of three, I learned to ski at two. My dad carried me down the hill in front of our house, my tiny skis corralled between his.

"You okay, Chipmunk?" he asked as he raced down to the scene and called out to people on the nearby chairlift to alert the ski patrol and send help to our location. I'd always wanted a ride on a Ski Patrol's toboggan, I just never imagined it would be for an actual injury. They strapped me in tight and cozy, but the ride was not pleasant, just bumpy and painful.

I sang hymns to myself to take my mind off the pain, there inside the blanket, breathing my own hot breath. "O gentle presence, peace and joy and power . . ." The ride ended by the patrol office at the base lodge. The guys in the red jackets with white crosses executed a two-man carry of me into their first aid room, the carry I'd seen in my brother's Boy Scout booklet when he was earning his first aid badge.

Ski Patrol did a quick assessment of my leg, asking where it hurt while poking, prodding, and examining my ripped pink snow pants.

"She seems awfully calm for someone who just got plowed down by a man twice her size," one of them said to my dad. They seemed impressed that I wasn't screaming. I do remember sharp zings of pain and feeling very cold. I'd learned how to pray since I was young, to turn my thought away from the physical and dwell on what I knew to be true about myself spiritually, the me that had never been in an accident, the me that God knew. It was challenging to stay calm and not get swept away by fear.

The adults focused on what to do with me. They quickly determined this was an urgent matter that needed X-rays. I remember them talking about not having a splint because someone else had broken their leg earlier that day, so they fashioned a U-shaped splint out of cardboard and tape.

"We can call an ambulance, which will take about forty-five minutes," they explained to my dad, "or you could drive her to the nearby emergency room." I can just see my dad's face now, beaming with confidence as he imagined handling the winding mountain roads with ease in his 1967 white Alfa Romeo. Two strong ski patrolmen maneuvered me into the tiny sports car, watching that my cardboard splint didn't hit the door frame as they gently placed me on the red leather front seat.

Daddy drove as carefully as he could, but as you can imagine, the cardboard leg bouncing up and down from the sports car's low clearance over rutty Vermont winter roads didn't make for a comfortable drive. I held it together, scared and in pain, choosing as best I could to hold onto the idea that God was right there with me and I could rely on Him to hold my hand.

They admitted me in a rush of attention, my dad answering all the medical questions, as I was whisked down the hall in a metal wheelchair to get X-rayed in a cold room on a metal exam table. After all the flurry, we waited. I was thirsty. I wasn't used to the smell of sterile air. The sounds were foreign, and nothing felt cozy or comforting.

I yearned for something to feel normal. Again, I retreated inside — to what I knew and what was familiar and felt safe — I said a prayer we repeated at the end of every Sunday school class that ends with "Therefore I am not material; I am spiritual," which put my focus on my spiritual self instead of my body. Just saying the statement in my head and staying focused on my spiritual identity lessened the pain and gave me a sense of calm and assurance as we continued to wait.

The doctor motioned to my dad while glancing down at his chart. I watched Daddy walk across the linoleum floor of green and off-white squares, still in his ski pants. I didn't want to know what the doctor was saying and kept looking down, praying that there wasn't a problem and that everything would be okay. I was more scared of losing time with my dad than I was about my leg, since I only got one-on-one time with him once every three months.

The doctor invited me to come with them down the hall and look at the X-rays on three big light-boxes mounted on the wall at their eye level. I looked up from the wheelchair while the doctor pointed to different images of my shin.

"She sure was lucky. The way her ski pants looked, I was expecting a bigger break." We nodded, waiting for the rest of his assessment. "But see this?" He pointed with his pen to the second image showing a different angle. "This fracture is in line with the bone." My dad, showing his cards as a surgeon's son, asked, "So what do you recommend for a hairline fracture?"

Then came the news I didn't want to hear. "Well, there's good news and bad." *Ugh!* I closed my eyes and shook my head. "The good news is, you don't need a cast. The bad news is, you won't be skiing any more this season. You need to stay off the leg for four to six weeks." I silently screamed "No!" inside my head and clung to a different perspective that told a different story, one that reaffirmed my relationship with God and didn't include anything about me that was broken.

My internal dialog was interrupted by the doctor offering pain medication. I had never taken any medication before, and it seemed an odd gesture. I declined, feeling confident in what I'd always known. My dad questioned me about my decision and may have accepted the doctor's offer, just to play it safe, but I was sure I wouldn't take them. I was wheeled to the exit.

They handed me crutches to use as I stood up from the wheelchair. I declined those, too, much to the doctor's surprise and a stern reaffirmation of my condition. "You need to stay off your leg and let it heal. That means use crutches and don't walk on your leg."

This was a moment of choice for me. What would I stand on — my mom's or my dad's approach? My mom used proven spiritual treatment and had taught me to do the same, while my dad relied on proven medical treatment, being the son of a Harvard medical professor and a well-known Boston surgeon. This was the first time I'd ever had to make such a decision in a vacuum of spiritual support from an adult. How could I oppose my dad — and the doctor?

I could choose to rely on medical science and the examination of matter to find reality, or choose to rely on divine science and the examination of Spirit to find reality. This one choice prompted the larger question as to the very basis of my existence, though I'm not sure the thoughts came to me in that way at the time. Was I going to stand on what I knew to be true of my spiritual nature, as not broken under spiritual law, and do so in the face of the authority of medical advice and evidence telling me I couldn't stand? Could I rely on the truth as I knew it to support me and release me from the pain that stemmed from the material belief? Did I have the spiritual strength to overcome the fear? The bottom line was, did I see myself as a spiritual being or a material being? These existential questions stood before me as worthy opponents to battle with my sword of choice. It all came down to this moment.

It was normal to choose a spiritual approach to healing. My confidence was born naturally out of my past experiences of quick healings. But this time, I was on my own.

Growing up, where most people's first aid is medicine and second aid is prayer, our first aid was prayer and second aid was medicine. It was effective, scientific prayer, based on God's law, the way Jesus healed. My dad's attitude was, "If they're not healed in three days, I'm taking them to a doctor," referencing Jesus' three days between crucifixion and resurrection. "If it's good enough for Jesus, it's good enough for them!" Because my childhood healings occurred within three days, I didn't go to the doctor except for the required annual school checkup. I witnessed spiritual healing and mindset over and over with the family, and even my dad started asking for spiritual help when problems came up. His dad, the surgeon, had great respect for this scientific approach to prayer and way of healing.

I was brought up with spiritual, metaphysical, and mental training that many kids don't get. When a way of thinking shapes a life, everything is affected. My natural love of God and the metaphysical training to see beyond the five physical senses offered me a different view of reality. It was normal for me to question the evidence or limits presented by matter and material sense. Sitting at the exit of the hospital, I had the opportunity to stand on my own.

I got up from the wheelchair and with a little hesitation, but not much, walked to the car with very little pain. When the pain would rise up in my thinking, I chose to listen only to what my spiritual understanding told me was true. I knew that "A house divided cannot stand," (Mark 3:25) literally! I needed to stand up and walk, so I knew I couldn't be divided in what I believed was true about me. Some might call this stupid. Some might call it human will. Some might argue this from other angles. All I can say is that I leaned on my experience of past healings using this process of seeing myself spiritually, and I was free from pain for the most part.

Settled in the car, we set off for the place we were staying that night. That car ride was markedly different from just a few hours before. This time I was sure of myself, not waiting to be *told* if I was okay, I'd chosen the truth of me and *knew* I was okay. There was no fear and very little pain as a result. This was definitely the first time I'd faced such a big physical diagnosis on my own.

That night at my dad's friend's house, I was gently guided to a quiet room and soft bed, which hinted at comfort even though that seemed elusive to me at the moment. After navigating teeth-brushing and pajamas, I managed to maneuver my way onto the bed without too much trouble and propped up pillows to sit up and pray. I honestly can't remember all the specific things I thought about, but I do remember feeling clear about the fact that I was alone with God, the spiritual ideas I'd always turned to, and there was nobody else to help me. I remembered a line from a hymn, "God, my best, my ever friend," and said a prayer I said every night. "*Now I lay me down to sleep, I know that God his child will keep. I know that God his life is nigh, I live in Him, I cannot die. God is my health, I can't be sick, God is my strength, unfailing, quick. God is my all, I know no fear, since Life and Truth and Love is here.*"

I pictured God's view of me and chose to hold tight to that and not let any other ideas flood in. I didn't allow myself to go down the rabbit hole of fear and what-if scenarios and the doctor's prescribed timeline for healing. I was determined to see myself as whole and free. Then I got really quiet and just listened. I listened for God to tell me something — an angel thought. I wanted to feel reassured that it was all okay and I could let it go. I remember kind of mentally turning the problem over to God and letting Him handle it and take care of me the way He always had.

In the quiet and stillness of that little room, under the floral-print quilt, I felt loved and safe. Then I felt something shift in my leg — it felt like a click — I don't quite know how to describe it other than to say, at that moment, my leg felt solid and strong like something had shifted, and I knew I was healed. I snuggled down into the covers and fell peacefully asleep.

When my dad woke me in the morning, I jumped out of bed excited to go skiing. Clearly surprised, my dad cocked his head sideways with a question in his eyes, looking for confirmation, and then he smiled, knowing exactly what had happened, since he'd seen evidence of healing many times before. I was healed, and as a result, I got to go skiing that day with my dad!

~ ~ ~ ~ ~

I chose for myself to rely on the law of good. I didn't have to rely on my parents, a doctor, or a spiritual practitioner. I realized that seeing myself spiritually as God's child was both powerful and practical. I could trust the choice to go directly to God as an effective and reliable approach when facing any challenge. That was huge.

~ ~ ~ ~ ~

The fact is: God is always available. The law of good is always operating. We all have constant access to a spiritual perspective and a higher way of thinking, no matter the circumstances or people involved. We all have the power to choose.

The thought process I went through for that healing was based on how I was trained to pray as a very young student of divine Science, most commonly known as Christian Science, discovered in the late 1800s by Mary Baker Eddy, who wrote the definitive textbook on the subject, *Science and Health with Key to the Scriptures*. My prayer was simple, childlike reasoning, and it's the same healing process I use today to support myself and my clients, having been trained as a practitioner of divine Science while in college.

The skiing healing became a pivotal experience and gave me confidence to choose Love over fear, Spirit over matter. This pushed open wide the door of possibility. Choosing between two modes of healing gave me what felt like a superpower — the ability to make choices in other areas of life governed by societal norms or authority figures — to challenge ingrained thought and see a broader landscape, one filled with greater hope and possibility.

So much suffering is a result of a lack of understanding or society's ingrained way of thinking, both of which block people from seeing the choice available to them. I want you to feel free from the struggle of knowing where to turn when you're in pain. I want you to have a tool you can reach for in a moment of need — whatever that need may be.

This three-step method is your get-out-of-jail-free card, your spiritual Swiss Army knife

Facing all the challenges in health, finances, relationships, career, identity, and more, I've developed a simple three-step approach to this Science, and I'd like to share it with you: Look Up, Look In, Look Out. This Up-In-Out Way is a tool to help you to recognize the power of the All (which I reference as God, but please use whatever term you are comfortable with), a consistent way to access it and live by it, and the confidence to lean on the Infinite as a way of life, particularly when the going gets tough. This three-step method is your get-out-of-jail-free card, your spiritual Swiss Army knife to use when you feel stuck.

I want you to feel free — to feel empowered — to know you have a choice to move forward in your life, even when everything around you is screaming: *You're stuck. This is all you get. Your only choice is to accept it.*

Look Up, Look In, Look Out guided me to my dream job, our lost son, and every place I've ever lived, protected me from accidents, saved a friend, and healed me from the trauma of abuse. In this book, you'll hear these and other ways Up-In-Out has given me freedom. I'll show you a life navigated by the compass of divine law and enough evidence so that you can decide for yourself whether this might be a compass for you. Let this be a spark of hope, a flashlight in the dark, that you, too, can choose to be governed by a higher law beyond worldly understanding.

I was tested that day on the slopes, and I found the spiritual strength to lift and wield this weighty sword of choice and slay the fear. I won my freedom. We can all do this. Knowing we have this choice opens a place of strength. Choice becomes a way of thinking, the fabric of our being. Anyone can choose good as the foundation, where health and harmony are the norm. Abundance is the norm. Where the law of good, seen through the lens of Up-In-Out, brings healing to every aspect of life.

The question is: What will you choose as the basis of your thought? Spirit or matter, internal or external, intuition or evidence, Self or self? The choice you make determines the experience you will have. When you choose a life based on your ego and fear, external measures and validation, you get limitations and suffering. When you choose a life based on your true self, aligned with God, love, internal measures and validation, you get more possibility, more abundance, more synchronicities, more freedom, more expansion and progress, more evidence of good in every area of life.

There's a reason you're here right now with this book. You were drawn to it. It has the answer to your heart's questions. You were drawn by a power larger than your ego, drawn here by the All-power, the force governing the pull on your heart.

Let this be the moment your life changes direction, the moment that all possibility opens for you, and use the simple framework offered in these pages, Look Up, Look In, Look Out, as a staff to lean on while you navigate the rough terrain of life on this planet. When you can *see* who you are, you can *be* who you are. Choose to be you. Your best life doesn't happen by *chance*. It happens by *choice*. This choice matters!

 PART 1

Learning to Listen

To listen. To hear. To tune in. To know what we're listening for. To recognize what we hear. To understand and trust the message. One of the key takeaways from this book is the ability to recognize the source of the voice inside our heart, the nudge that guides us towards good. If you know it well enough and act on it consistently, what unfolds will amaze you.

At the heart of learning to listen is the question, what are we listening to? Can we hear the power of good governing all? The force that aligns and balances all? The power that created us and put the desire inside us to be who we are?

Are we willing to trust this power to guide and govern us to fulfill our purpose? When we do, we will move through the world with the power of good as the basis of our life and reality. We will trust this All-power to speak to us in a whisper, in a still small voice, in an intuition, an inspiration, an angel message, a synchronicity, a sign, a spirit moved, a healing. Learn to listen to God's guidance and your whole life will change for the better.

CHAPTER 1

Listen and Follow

And thine ears shall hear a word behind thee, saying,
This is the way, walk ye in it, when ye turn to the
right hand, and when ye turn to the left.
— Isaiah 30:21

It was 2:00 in the morning. I heard the drone of the janitor's vacuum humming in a distant hallway, a sure sign they'd be closing the building any moment. More studying wasn't going to make exams go better; what I really needed was some sleep. Heading out the door of the School of Government building into the expanse of life beyond books, thoughts lofted into the still night air and lighted gently on the branches of possibility, and with a yawn, were quickly yanked back to imagining my pillow. It was only a five-minute walk to my cozy bed in the Andy East dorm on the northside of campus.

After a few steps, an intuition came loud and clear: "Go to Cox Cottage!"

"Why would I go to the infirmary? I'm not sick; I'm just tired! And, it's on the other side of campus," I argued in my head, continuing towards my dorm.

"Go to Cox!" The intuition insisted.

I made a pact with God when I was six that I'd always follow the voice inside, even if it didn't seem to make sense. This made no sense at all! I embraced the contradiction, turned around, and headed south while shaking my head no.

"I'll go, but I'm not sick."

It was a twenty-minute walk to Cox, and I was fried.

"I must be nuts."

But this is what it looked like to listen and follow against what circumstances would dictate. Oddly, heading to Cox made me feel calm and clear. My exhaustion lifted. I knew that the infirmary door got locked at 11:00 p.m., and students had to ring to gain entrance after hours.

"I'm not ringing the buzzer!" I protested, head down, watching my footing as I walked through the apple trees along the dimly lit, winding footpath. With every step in the darkness, certainty grew that I was doing the right thing, but I still just wanted to get this over with. I walked as fast as I could, half hoping to get another intuition to go back to my dorm. That intuition never came. Twenty minutes later, I stood at the door of Cox, stared at the little placard above the white buzzer [Door Locked at 11:00 p.m., Ring Buzzer], crossed my arms, and looked up.

"I'm not ringing the buzzer!"

Clear and strong the voice came, "Try the doorknob."

I shrugged in submission and reached out. I turned the cool metal doorknob slowly, trying to be quiet.

Strange, I thought, *it's unlocked.*

I swung the door open, stepping tentatively into the unlit entryway, hoping not to wake anyone. Then I noticed a sound coming from the back of the cottage. Someone was crying. Following the echoes of distress through darkened halls, I headed toward a glow of light.

I ended up back in the kitchen. And there, on the floor, was the nurse, unable to get up, sobbing. She seemed to be in great pain and looked up with tears in her eyes, "How did you know to come? I've been praying that someone would come and help me."

In that moment, we felt the power and presence of something far larger than either of us. There was a palpable sense of love filling the space. I welled up with tears, unable to contain my gratitude for the message that had led me there.

I carefully helped her to a bed, and she asked if I would stay with her and pray. I sat by her bedside singing hymns and reading spiritual truths. She fell into a peaceful sleep. I stayed by her side and continued to pray. She woke the next morning well enough for me to hand her care over to the day nurse as I went on to exams feeling oddly rested.

Intuition guides us to fulfill divine Love's plan, not ours

This experience was one of those dramatic confirmations that following intuition never fails, and internal spiritual guidance surpasses human reasoning. When we listen to those gentle, knowing prompts, it always leads to more good. This experience was also a reminder that intuition doesn't necessarily give us the whole picture or align with immediate circumstances, but we can trust we're being guided to a good end. Choosing to follow intuition isn't about ensuring our own life gets better; often, the calling is for someone else's benefit. Intuition guides us to fulfill divine Love's plan, not ours.

The nurse reached out to a power that would protect and guard her. She reached out to Love to meet her need. Love guided me to help the nurse. Following my intuition guided me to fulfill Love's plan, to walk a path of service. I've looked back on this example throughout my life whenever I've doubted that still, small voice. It was important for me to follow my intuition for that nurse. Isn't it just as important for us to follow our intuition in our own lives?

This story illustrates the core message of this book: we all have a choice in every moment to either base our life on material evidence or spiritual intuition, that *each choice we make shapes the direction of our life, and that we can change the direction of our life with a choice*. When we choose to be guided by spiritual intuition, which some might call angels, inspiration, or God's thoughts, we put ourselves on a fast track of synchronicity and align our lives with a larger good than we can see humanly.

It's key for us to recognize our intuition and know how it shows up for us, so we can follow it intentionally instead of ignoring it or missing it all together. What do you need to look for? How do you know it's intuition? What does it sound like and feel like to you? Let's look at ways you can get to know that. We'll look at this specifically in a moment.

Based on my experience of following intuition for fifty-plus years, I can tell you that choosing a spiritual mindset, one that recognizes the power of God, rather than a limited material mindset, leads to better results — a life of more peace, abundance, health, harmony, love, joy, fulfillment, and good. *Cultivating a spiritual mindset, the mindset where intuition is clearly seen, is the most important practice we can ingrain in ourselves and our children.*

As a child, I learned that spiritual law governed reality, and when material sense presented me with limitations, I chose to see beyond them by utilizing my spiritual sense. I chose to focus on the spiritual instead of the material, which gave me freedom. I understood that spiritual law or divine law was always operating, and that I could lean on it whenever I faced problems. By understanding spiritual law, we gain another option and have a choice. Without understanding spiritual law, options are limited to what can be seen on the surface. Intuition and spiritual sense give us access to the higher reality — spiritual reality — and cultivating a spiritual mindset is the first step.

If you haven't yet cultivated a spiritual mindset, don't wait. Begin now. More good will appear in your life when choices are based on a spiritual mindset. If everyone lived their life this way, our world would flow in the rhythm of Love, and we would experience more peace and harmony, abundance and fulfillment, balance and integration. As the Bible says, "All things work together for good to them that love God."

So let's get practical. What elements are included in a spiritual mindset? What are the elements that allow us to tune in to spiritual intuition and perception, and deep knowing beyond physical evidence? What are the qualities of thought needed to make each choice in the context of this spiritual awareness?

When I speak of spiritual mindset, I mean a mindset based in an understanding of God and divine Reality, but if you're not comfortable with the word God, please plug in whatever works for you, whether it be Creator, Truth, Mother Nature, Love, Buddha, the Higgs Field, the Universe, Source, Life, Allah, the Om, the Big Magic . . . it really doesn't matter. The point is, there is a power governing all of existence and creation. There is a power or intelligence beyond us that formed who we are, that conceived of our individual nature and uniqueness. An intelligence governing us, governing life — our heartbeat and breath. An intelligence we can turn to or tune in to that knows all and with which we can find a way forward — an answer.

A spiritual mindset, then, is the use of spiritual sense — seeing good, tapping in to divine power and intelligence, aligning with it, feeling it, listening to it, and being at one with the All that is.

Elements of Intuition

Before the Cox Cottage experience, I was used to hearing intuition and trusting it, having had many experiences prior to this that gave me confidence in what I heard. So, let's pull this apart a little and look at the different elements of intuition.

Any thinking based in fear and limitation will block your intuition.

Notice in this experience that I recognized the thought as intuition — the thought just appeared. It came in the form of a voice in my head from out of nowhere, an idea that was not from my thinking place.

So, the first step is to know how intuition shows up for you. What does it sound, feel, or look like? In what form does intuition appear for you? Does it appear as a thought, a picture, a feeling, words or sounds, a knowing, signs, conversations around you? Perhaps it comes from more unexpected places like license plates or an image on a billboard. Working with clients, it is clear that intuition comes in many forms and is as varied as the individuals.

Even so, there are qualities of intuition and patterns to note. Let's look at it through the Cox Cottage experience to get a clearer picture of how you can evaluate intuition and learn to separate the chaff from the wheat.

- The thought that came to me was emotionally neutral. It was strong and clear, but not pushy or bossy, and at the same time, powerful, certain.

- I interacted with the intuitive thought. I made a choice to listen to it and then after a little bit of debate, decided to follow it. This was a clear choice for me because of the foundation of my past experiences, but for someone new to this, it might feel a bit scary to have an intuition and follow it, especially when it goes against what common sense is telling you to do. (Side note here — obviously, I'm not suggesting that you unthinkingly and blindly follow an intuition if by following it you'd be putting yourself in danger.) I can say without reservation that every time I've followed a spiritual intuition, it has never led me into personal danger or loss of good.

- Many times along the way, intellectual reasoning has argued with intuitive guidance and attempted to talk me out of following it.

Those not practiced in this art may give in to the arguments and justify changing course and turning away from the guidance. Again, this is where practice and experience give you the confidence to follow intuition in the face of opposing reason and evidence. At first, I resisted what I was being asked to do, and yet, each time the resistance came up, I overrode it with a deeper awareness of what was going on, yielded to the voice's demands, and took action. Each time I felt doubt, I was guided to a clear path and found confirmation that I was doing the right thing.

- Intuition many times does not give us the whole answer at once. First I was told to go to Cox, then I was told to try the doorknob, then I was guided to follow the sound. I was not told, "There's a nurse on the floor of the kitchen in Cox who needs your help, go help her." We can trust that each step we're given is the right step. The information we need will come when we need it, not necessarily when we want it.

- Do you know the voice of your intuition? Are you ready to become aware of it? Prior to getting in the habit of noticing your intuitive voice, you may need to practice listening to your inner knowing. Some would call it the still, small voice or the voice of your higher self or conscience. Others might call it the voice of God. A good way to start tuning in to this part of you is to practice. Here's a method that has helped many of my clients.

Set a timer for seven minutes each day and sit comfortably in stillness and quiet with no distractions. Allow your thoughts to pass by, and without judging them, notice that they're there. Let them be as clouds floating by. Then notice that you are observing the thoughts. You are the observer, and the voice of the observer is the one closer to your inner voice. Get familiar with that voice. It may come through more as a feeling than words.

Don't worry if you struggle with the practice to begin with. Getting quiet enough to be the one observing the thoughts can take practice. The to-do list is a big distraction. Agree with yourself that you'll do nothing but listen for those seven minutes. Give yourself permission to be singular in your intent and practice. Multitasking is not your friend during this exercise.

Continue to practice listening and tuning in to your inner voice. As your practice develops, you can build on that foundation. Notice who you are when you hear your inner voice. What qualities are you expressing? Peace? Stillness? Calm? You'll want to cultivate these qualities so that you are available to hear your intuition or the voice of higher knowing, the voice of God, or the Holy Spirit. Practice expressing these qualities throughout your day and tuning in. Then notice what gets in the way of hearing your intuition. Generally, it will be intellectual reasoning or egoic, monkey-mind thoughts that leap from branch to branch. Any thinking based in fear and limitation will block your intuition. Notice whether thoughts are based on a limited or expansive perspective. Practice releasing or being released from the ego's view and commit to seeing the higher plan.

Here's how your view can shift in an instant. Imagine you are looking through a telescope and all you see is what's in the scope's narrow field of view. You are unaware of the countless stars or planets beyond that limited perspective. Now take your eye off the eye-piece and look up at the sky to the vastness of infinite space and an ever-expanding universe. Your perspective matters. Are you looking through a limited, material lens or through an unlimited, spiritual one?

If you're looking only at matter, your entire reality is based on what can be observed materially. Your experience will be limited, finite, mortal, material.

If you're looking at what seems to be a mixture of matter and Spirit, your reality is based on what can be observed both materially and spiritually. Your experience will be proportionally expansive or limited depending on the lens you choose — varying amounts of good and bad, love and fear, connection and separation, willingness and resistance, etc.

If you're looking only at Spirit, your entire reality is based on what you observe spiritually. Your experience will be unlimited, infinite, immortal, spiritual.

If you want to be guided by a higher law, you need to look out from a higher perspective — that of Spirit — and see and sense the spiritual nature of everyone and everything around you. That means choosing to utilize your spiritual senses.

What qualities would we need to express humanly in order to engage spiritual sense? That's what we're talking about. What can we do to cultivate that place in us that is receptive to perceiving spiritually?

- Be at peace.

- Be still inside and cultivate mental stillness. Being physically still can help get you there mentally, but there are times when it is not possible to be physically still, so we need to cultivate an ability to find stillness in the middle of surrounding chaos or activity.

- Be aware of your own thoughts and recognize the thoughts are not who you are.

- Be calm.

- Be emotionally neutral.

- Be humble.

- Be open and curious.

- Be free of judgment of yourself and others and situations.

- Be loving of yourself and others.

- Be present and aware.

- Be your true, transparent, authentic self.

- Be expectant only of good and confident that good is all there is in reality.

CHAPTER 2

We Are Led Step by Step

*Take the first step in faith. You don't have to see
the whole staircase, just take the first step.*
— Dr. Martin Luther King Jr.

Right out of college, I felt pressured to get a job quickly! I'd
worked at The Center, the world headquarters of the Christian
Science church in Boston during college breaks, so I started
looking there. First stop, the Film and Television department, to
combine my love for the church and my passion for the arts. There
were no jobs available. The reasoned, practical approach didn't yield
a job. I switched my approach, listened for and yielded to guidance
from above, and was willing to serve. My thought was open to hear
intuition and fresh ideas to follow.

Intuition prompted me to walk through the garage at The Center,
not a typical way to enter the building. And there I ran into the sister
of a college friend who happened to work in personnel.

"You know, there is a job opening in the marketing department,"
she said as we talked. "Why don't you give it a look?" It was a match.
Intuition led me to my first full-time job out of college. I was hired as
secretary for the manager of the marketing department at CSPS (the
Christian Science Publishing Society), home of the Pulitzer Prize-
winning newspaper *The Christian Science Monitor.*

I loved starting my adult life. I lived in my first apartment on my
own. I was free to envision and create the life of my dreams. But I felt
divine guidance had really steered me wrong. Although I had great
rapport with both of my bosses that year, I *really* didn't feel in my
element doing secretarial work. Loved the people, loved the cause I

was working for, did not love the work. I grew increasingly frustrated and wanted something that utilized my skills and lit me up inside. I wanted something fulfilling, enriching, inspiring, and creative. I had a desire to communicate the truth. How could I have been guided to this? I wanted more.

I turned to a short newspaper clipping, "Right for Me" by Alex Noble, in which she says, "The question, 'Do I feel happy about this?' is not a frivolous one." So I asked myself, "What makes me happy?"

This self-inquiry took me down several roads and ultimately felt more confusing than helpful. So the answer to this moment, sitting at my desk, swiveling in my chair, was again turning inward to my heart and getting out of my head. Where was my heart leading me? The answer seemed odd at the time. The thoughts that poured in were about flying. I had no idea why, but I went with it. I let the thoughts flow.

I love to fly. Even as a passenger — love being untethered and in that floating place where gravity and time are suspended and everything is possible, feeling immortal from the point of liftoff to the moment of touchdown. Being in the cocoon, the chosen cone of silence amidst constant white noise and voices. I imagined that someday I'd learn to fly. I thought of my favorite uncle, Uncle Walt, a VP at Pan Am Airlines, and the many pilots in our extended family. One even flew Air Force jets. It was possible.

Thoughts about flying hung there suspended like planes do. I decided to follow this intuition and find out what it would take to learn to fly.

The process of following intuition takes many different turns; at that point I trusted what I was naturally being led to do. Listen, trust, act. Look Up. Look In. Look Out. Synchronicities led me to conversations, people, and information that furthered my interest and intuition. The movie, *An Officer and a Gentleman*, had come out the previous year. I grew up on the ocean, sailing, diving off the rocks or jumping off bridges, swimming at the beach, and fishing off my dad's powerboats. I loved the water, and through windsurfing, had a growing penchant for speed. A mash-up of these interests and

WE ARE LED STEP BY STEP

influences naturally, I say with a bit of tongue in cheek, brought the next question. What about flying jets for the Navy?

I applied to the Naval Aviation Officer Candidate School (AOCS) and figured if I'm going to learn to fly, I want to fly jets, and the best trained pilots are those who can land on what looks like a postage stamp bobbing in the water.

The process was challenging and lengthy. There were many tests: physical, mental, and academic. It took months, all while I sat at my desk playing secretary in the marketing department at the Publishing Society in Boston. I felt somewhat comforted by the fact that I was working toward a different future than where I found myself.

And I waited. I did the best I could as a secretary, learning all I could about office life and what was expected of me, but I became increasingly depressed.

One day, completely despondent that nothing had changed, the Navy application in a holding pattern, I yearned for life to shift. I struggled to accept my present circumstances. Where was the robust life filled with passion that my college-self had imagined? Friends, activities, travel, a feeling of fulfillment and utility. Would that life ever be realized? Would the passion for life inside of me be fully expressed?

I knew the discontent would not go away on its own and that finding an answer was an inside job and would not come from a change of circumstances. I called a spiritual practitioner for guidance. I needed to get unstuck from finding an external solution (the job title and salary and to-do list), and move to finding the internal solution (who I was being and the spiritual qualities I was expressing while doing the job). Did the job bring out the best in me? Did I express contentment, patience, and joy, or frustration, anxiety, and fear? I needed to find the solution in who I was rather than in what I did.

The practitioner gave me one simple directive with utter confidence, "Don't lift a pencil or do anything until you can do it with love." This was a directive to Look Up — for me to place a higher priority on expressing the quality of love than meeting my personal need for fulfillment by doing something.

The good worker in me rebelled instantly, knowing that would mean I'd look like a bad employee. Hmmm . . . that meant no filing, no labeling, no busy work, no work that made me feel underutilized? I sat for long stretches, unable to do anything, because I couldn't honestly do it with love.

This forced me to focus outward. I expressed love while greeting people as they entered the office, answering the phone and serving others, typing and writing ideas, and offering creative solutions to problems. I got some tasks done, but it was a rocky road and all felt mundane and pointless. It wasn't leading me to work that allowed me to grow and shine.

By lunchtime that day, I left the office in tears, truly at the breaking point. I couldn't last another minute! I refused to believe this was my lot and I'd have to suck it up and live with it. I wanted an answer, something concrete I could hold on to; I wanted to know my life would change for the better. The times in my life when I'd followed intuition always seemed to work out better. I yearned to feel guided — some confirmation that there was more for me!

the desire to feel released from the pressure was greater than the resistance to giving up control

I walked out at lunch onto the wide-open I. M. Pei-designed plaza, took a deep breath, and the tears flowed. I didn't hold back for fear of being seen by office mates. I made my way to the end of a reflecting pool and settled on the concrete bench by a fountain.

Despondency pushed me to go to the deeper place within — that desire in me to serve a higher purpose, which genuinely had always been to serve God. I just didn't know what that looked like at that moment. That egoic place in me that was clinging to what the *little I* wanted, had only one thing to do — yield. The struggle and pain of that moment stemmed from my ego's resistance to yielding control.

But the desire to feel released from the pressure was greater than the resistance to giving up control. The only way out of pain was to claim my desire to serve God and let that desire be primary. I was willing to do anything God wanted me to do and yearned to be utilized fully. I looked up.

"I'm here to serve you. What do you want me to do? I'll do whatever you say. I'll sweep floors at McDonalds if that's what you want. Just tell me what I'm supposed to do! The answer needs to be as obvious as an elephant standing on my foot!" I implored. I reached out with my whole heart. I listened.

I heard a voice behind me say, "You'll be in Boston for a while."

I turned around, expecting to see who spoke. No one was there. "That's not an answer!" I argued. "I need to know what you want me to do!" Then I stopped myself. "I said I'd do whatever you say. That's my answer."

The answer didn't make sense — other than the obvious point of staying in Boston — so I trusted that was my answer, got up from where I was sitting, and started walking across the brick plaza back to the office. About twenty paces later, out from the pillars of the cement colonnade building came my old boss who had moved to a different office a few months earlier.

"Where are you these days, Lisa?" He knew I'd been struggling.

"Funny you should ask, John. I just got a really clear sense that I'll be in Boston for a while."

"I'm really glad to hear you say that. Come upstairs, I want to offer you a job."

John presented the opportunity to be part of a new radio division. It would be a few select people who would flesh out the vision, design the program, and build a team. It sounded amazing. I floated back to my office.

Wait. The story gets better. As I approached my desk, the phone rang. It was Dave, the head of the current radio division. He asked if I wanted to fill in for someone going on vacation, writing stories for Radio News Service and voicing them for broadcast. It was a chance to see if I was a good fit for the job and if it was a good fit for me. I called John.

"John, Dave just called and offered me a job in Radio News Service."

"Tell him you'll call back later today. He's about to find out about the new direction being taken."

This was about as obvious a sign as I could have hoped for — getting two broadcasting job offers from two different people within minutes of each other. It would be a month before the new division started up, and in the meantime, I was to work in Radio News Service, which amounted to a crash course in broadcasting. I reached deep and utilized talents that came naturally: listening, editing, writing at speed, synthesizing, and working with an intensity that made me feel alive and purposeful.

So now what would I do about the Navy? I'd been guided by intuition to apply, and the process was still ongoing. By the time the new radio division was up and running, I still hadn't heard. I needed to trust. You know the way we don't always get all the information at once with intuition? This was a perfect example. Both these opportunities were running in tandem, and both were lives I could envision for myself. Then the letter came, the embossed Navy seal prominent on the envelope.

Remember when you applied for college, and the letter meant rejection and the packet meant acceptance? This was a single-page letter, three short paragraphs, so I prepared for rejection. Only five women in the country had been accepted into the Navy's AOCS that year, it said. My eyes widened as I read; I was one of them! It was made crystal clear that this was a once-in-a-lifetime opportunity.

To accept, I was to follow detailed instructions on next steps. Set up a meeting with the recruiter to get all the information. Make another appointment to sign the contract and begin the six-year journey of commitment and service to my country. The name of my contact and date and time of the first appointment were noted. I was to call and confirm, which of course I did.

Then the battle of reasoning began. Intuition had guided me down two distinct paths. And now both were converging, and only one would be the path I walked.

Only a few months into my work in broadcasting, I felt challenged and utilized, fulfilled and happy, completely aligned with all that was being asked of me. With reporters, producers, and staff working closely together, we designed and planned for our first edition of *MonitoRadio*, the weekly hour-long public radio news program of the *Christian Science Monitor*. It was exciting, and every day brought new challenges and wins.

be patient and humble and willing to follow
without knowing the big picture

With the deadline for signing the Navy contract approaching, the wheels of decision-making went into high gear — steam and grinding noises, labored and loud, reverberated inside my head. And that's where I stayed stuck — in my head. Though my heart had guided me to these two paths, my head had taken over.

I made lists of pros and cons. I imagined day-to-day life in both jobs as best I could. How would each job mold me? What skills would I acquire, and what new career prospects would open up? All the usual questions. But what were my next steps? Nothing was clear. The more I thought it through, the more muddled things got. And then, as though God Himself was playing a cosmic joke, the date I was to sign the Navy contract was the exact day we were scheduled to record the very first edition of *MonitoRadio*. Priceless! Really?! I needed to know which path was right.

The ego didn't want to let go, and as we know, resistance equates to pain. Many tears later and with a depth of anguish that my few years of experience couldn't put in perspective, I finally turned the whole thing over to God. This was bigger than I could handle. It was too important with too many elements I just couldn't see from my vantage point. I got very still and quiet. That's a good sign and is often the first step in the sometimes long and arduous journey from head to heart. This process again followed what I now simply call Up-In-Out.

I yearned to serve a higher cause beyond self. I Looked Up, turned it over to God, the all-knowing Mind. I asked for a clear answer that would satisfy my desire to be of service in a way that aligned with who I was. I Looked In with all my heart. Did the answer feel right and align with my highest self? And then by releasing the outcome with a service mindset, I Looked Out, waited to be shown the answer, and let the guidance take shape.

We all have this built-in divine GPS (God Positioning System), telling us the next turn.

A line from John Greenleaf Whittier rang in my ears, "In purer lives Thy service find." That was it. I had my answer. Falling on other ears, it may have pointed to a different path, but for me it translated into working for the *Monitor* in broadcasting. As much as I loved the idea of flying jets, there was no guarantee I'd make it through training, and ultimately, if I made it through, it was all in preparation to go to war. As it turns out, had I become an officer, I would have been smack dab in the middle of the Gulf War, which broke out about five years later. Shortly after that, the TailHook Scandal shed light on "a hostile attitude in US military culture towards women in the areas of sexual harassment, sexual assault, and equal treatment of women in career advancement and opportunity."

The path was clear, and the Navy was none-too-pleased when I turned them down. Had the intuition not landed with conviction, saying no to the Navy would have felt like I was losing something; instead, I'd gained a deeper understanding of myself and the intuition that guided me. I watched the pieces of my puzzle life get placed for me over and over again. I was moved into new positions about five times during those ten years at the *Monitor,* and each time, I used the same process of Up-In-Out — serve God, align with my heart, trust and follow, and let go of the outcome. Being guided by that still, small voice took many forms: I got on the elevator at the perfect time, made a call to the right person, or spoke up about an interest or skill I had, all of which put me in exactly the right place to serve in a bigger way. I trusted this guidance, and the intuition of the moment always led me to the next best action.

I followed even when the answer didn't satisfy my desire for details. Sometimes intuition came in pieces, little messages with just the amount of information I needed to take the next step. We all have this built-in divine GPS (God Positioning System), telling us the next turn. We may want to know the big picture, but we must learn to trust we're being given everything we need at the perfect time.

All the little pieces fit together exactly. I was guided to work in marketing, which seemed completely contrary to the path I wanted. But I worked directly for the man who later started the new radio division and for the woman who later became the executive producer of the whole broadcast arm of the *Monitor*. Though that desk didn't feel like the right place for me, it was a necessary step. We get confirmation of rightness when we look back and see all the pieces fit together and create the seamless picture. This gives us confidence to trust we're being guided even when the outward evidence doesn't immediately confirm our vision.

The other part to notice here is *being* versus *doing*. Who I wanted to be and the qualities I would express were more important than what I'd be doing in the job itself. The goal was to be my true God-like self, fully expressed, in whatever I was asked to do. At the time, that's not what it felt like. I was focused on knowing what God wanted me to do! When I got the unexpected answer at the fountain, I didn't get what I'd asked for, but I got what I needed — to be patient and humble and willing to follow without knowing the big picture.

To summarize this chapter: Get to know how your intuition shows up for you, how God talks to you. Understand the characteristics of an intuitive idea versus an egoic idea. Am I listening to the still, small voice and humbly following that, like when the answer came in that quote, *in purer lives thy service find?* Or am I willfully following what my ego wants with no thought of serving a higher ideal? Check in with yourself to see how much you trust your intuition and if you're willing to follow it. Recognize that intuition works on its own timeline.

Sometimes the slow drip of intuitive nudges requires patience to see the big picture. Many times we don't see how all the pieces fit together until we look back. Also, take a moment to notice the Up-In-Out approach stays the same no matter how much information is revealed each time. Look Up to your higher power, Look In to see if it aligns with your heart and highest self, and Look Out to trust the intuition and take a step to act on it.

EXERCISE

Once you've cultivated the way of being that is ripe to receive angels, intuition, what are some things to help you recognize intuition so you can become aware of how it shows up for you (auditory, visual, sensory, knowing, etc.)?

- Notice that intuition comes in peace and brings calm.

- Notice that intuition is neutral and carries no emotional charge.

- Notice that intuition is clear and definite, singular.

- It's important to notice what intuition *is not*. It comes with no judgment or emotion, no fear or doubt, no limitation, no manipulation, and no time — though sometimes the intuition has urgency.

- Notice that it is not willful or full of egoic thinking or outlining.

- Practice following intuition with little things to gain confidence.

- Trust that you are being guided and are given what you need, when you need it.

- Recognize that intuition may contradict human reasoning or material evidence, and notice what thoughts you would need to overcome to follow your intuition.

- Notice that good is the only result because the All-knowing is the source of spiritual intuition, and All is Love.

The good news is everyone has intuition — the divine voice within. And once you become aware of what it sounds and feels like, you can begin to practice using it, hear or feel it, follow it, and rely on it in all areas of your life. You will build on your understanding each time you experience intuition or inspiration and are guided. You'll feel more comfortable with it the more you practice using it. Be patient with yourself, and be patient with intuition too. The guidance you seek may not arrive all at once.

✸ CHAPTER 3 ✸

Learning to Balance Intuition and Reason

Into His haven of Soul there enters no element of earth to cast out angels, to silence the right intuition which guides you safely home.
— Mary Baker Eddy

I met Jeff and Wendy the summer before ninth grade. They were the chaperones on the Greyhound bus I took (along with twenty-eight other teenagers, including my brother and sister), from Boston to the Adventure Unlimited Ranches in Buena Vista, Colorado. The three-day trek ended on Country Road 366 under an enormous wooden entry sign that still reads, *Welcome Home.* Jeff and Wendy were newly married, only twenty-one and twenty-two years old, and it wasn't always obvious who the chaperones were.

I was one of the youngest ones on the bus but felt most comfortable with and made a beeline to Jeff and Wendy. We had long talks about metaphysics, and I relished a male perspective and energy, having been starved of that since my parents' divorce six years before. We became fast friends that summer and grew closer that year during weekend visits to their home in Marblehead.

When they moved to Colorado Springs, they invited me to stay with them the following summer. My mom didn't relish the idea of me living two thousand miles from home with the young couple when I was only fifteen. I Looked Up and listened for guidance. When I Looked In, I put aside what I wanted and asked if it felt right to go. It did. Mummy knew that I was determined to follow whatever felt intuitively right to me. I had been doing so for years. She let me go and trusted me to God.

I didn't believe age was a legitimate
measure of skill or maturity

It was a summer of lessons. I had lots of independence, living with two people who weren't parents, but when I listened to God and followed my intuition, it bumped up against Jeff and Wendy's measure of normal behavior. They had taken on the responsibility of a teenager who acted like a peer. I learned to communicate more of my intuition to them and be transparent with my thought processes so they'd see that I wasn't going into things blindly. There was a learning curve on both sides.

With lots of time on my hands to Look Up and know God, Look In and know my true self as a divine reflection, it was time to Look Out. At fifteen, I didn't believe age was a legitimate measure of skill or maturity, so I got two jobs. I worked as the stage manager for Colorado College, where all my theater experience literally paid dividends by increasing my bank account and swelling my spirit. I also worked as a phone solicitor for the Jaycees, selling tickets to a circus, and where they fired you on the spot if you didn't meet the sales quota during your four-hour shift. I lasted all summer.

I looked into working at the local Top 40 radio station in Colorado Springs and rode my bike downtown to meet the DJ. This didn't feel far-fetched to me because WRKO, the popular Top 40 station back home, hired high school reporters to do humorous bits over the phone. I called in a lot and had fun bantering with the DJ, Bob Adams; my mom had even driven me into the city to meet him. But in Colorado Springs, I was on my own, and by the time I was done meeting with the DJ, it was getting dark. Not an ideal scenario to ride a bike. He offered to take me home but said he needed to make a few stops along the way.

Intuitively, it didn't feel right to get into the car with someone I didn't know, but calling Jeff and Wendy and telling them what I'd done felt more imposing than accepting the ride. So I overrode the intuition and went anyway. I let my fear of looking irresponsible to my friends govern my decision — rather than listening to my still small voice — which of course would backfire later.

I was in a car with a stranger, and nobody knew where I was. I didn't even know where I was! He did indeed make multiple stops along the way, including drinking with his friends while I waited outside. When I overheard their conversation reference me, the way I looked, that nobody knew where I was, that they could do anything and nobody would know, and talked about different ways they could take advantage of me, I felt scared and finally took charge of my thinking.

I Looked Up, reached out to God to feel safe. The Bible says God is Love so Love was there with me. I Looked In to feel loved and cared for, innocent and guided. I Looked Out to see that the DJ and his friends were also reflections of God, Mind, and therefore had good thoughts and would respond to good, another name for God. With this Up-In-Out way of reasoning, my mindset shifted.

Rather than thinking the worst of him and feeling like he could be the source of trouble, I started seeing him as kind and considerate and was grateful he offered the ride. As soon as my thought shifted, his conversation went from referencing me as an annoyance and ways they could all mess with me, to suggesting that he drive me home and then come back to hang out. I went from feeling like a victim of circumstance to taking individual responsibility for what I was holding in thought. But the lesson wasn't over.

Getting a ride home with an older stranger didn't go over well with Jeff. He gave me the silent treatment for three days until I acknowledged what I'd done, explained how I reasoned through my choices, and agreed to do it differently next time. I needed to respect them enough to communicate fully and demonstrate maturity. I admitted that I'd let my fear of their judgment govern my decision and promised I wouldn't do that again.

It was good to know that even though the bad circumstance was a result of my own bad decision, I was still able to turn to God for help, which resolved the situation harmoniously for everyone involved.

Aside from seeing the effect of Look Up, Look In, Look Out, though I didn't call it that then, I learned two very important lessons about following intuition that summer. One, be wise in your approach; if you don't know the level of safety in a situation, at least know the facts from a broader perspective in order to balance intuition and reason. And two, silence is a much more powerful deterrent than loud condemnation.

Intuition is calm and knowing, where ego is often pushy and fringed with pride

I carried both these lessons forward with me into many other difficult situations when intuition led me into uncharted waters. Without the parental bumpers, I bowled a lot of gutter balls that summer and very few strikes, but I did hone my ability to hear intuition. I also became very alert to the zealous teen desire to "go do stuff," which at times masqueraded as intuition, and I learned to discern the difference. Intuition and ego sound different. Intuition is calm and knowing, where ego is often pushy and fringed with pride.

It was as though I learned these lessons in the reverse order. I learned to trust my own intuition before I learned to balance my intuition with reasoned adult perspective.

CHAPTER 4

Listening or Deciding?

Intuition is a faith in the invisible forces of the world.
It is the wisdom that goes beyond reason.
— Ralph Waldo Emerson

What do you do when you're guided by intuition, but the whole map isn't laid out before you? Do you trust that you'll be given the step after this one? Do you listen and follow, knowing that you're being guided? Or do you wait for more information before going forward?

It's important to see the nature of spiritual intuition, inspiration, or divine knowing. It is a present-tense reality. Meaning, it only exists in the present. Therefore, when we're truly aligned with the All-knowing, we know all we need to know in this moment. We don't need to be aware of anything in the next moment-of-now. And there's the tricky part for the egoic mind. It wants to know the future (which doesn't exist in reality). It wants to make sense of the past or hang on to past hurts, traumas, and disappointments (which also don't exist in reality).

The future and the past only exist insofar as we allow them to hold space in our present conscious awareness. So if we trust enough to let go of holding the past or future in the now-of-consciousness, we are free from it. And to do that, what do we trust? Trust that the all-knowing Mind is always reflected by us as individuals, and therefore, in every now-moment, we can trust that we include every idea we need right now, and we can let go of every idea we think we want. So the battle isn't between what we know or don't know in the moment; the battle is between recognizing or not — that we are the very expression of the All-knowing and can't get away from that fact.

The question is, from which premise do we act? Do we reflect divine knowing? Or do we ourselves need to know? Do we trust that we are the expression of the All-knowing — reflected or manifested — and that we know all we need each moment? Or do we personally need to know more? Trust and take a step, or distrust and wait to know more?

when you solidify your relationship with divine Love itself and Look In, your human relationships naturally improve

I dropped my kids at school and contemplated what to do next. Sitting outside the school gate about to turn onto Mulholland Drive, I paused. Should I turn left and drive to my friend Mel's house, or turn right and go home and paint the living room? Instead of *deciding*, I thought I would *listen* for the answer. I followed Look Up, Look In, Look Out. This is a good example of tuning in to intuition when the stakes were low and either choice would've been fine. I also knew from experience that when I listen to an *angel* — a spiritual intuition — instead of my own ego, I'm never steered wrong, and I'm led to the action that will serve the highest good.

I closed my eyes and tuned out all the reasoning clamoring for my attention. I quieted the pros and cons that would keep me in a decision-making loop. I got peaceful and stayed in a neutral mental space without holding onto my own opinion about what to do. I listened for my next step.

To Look Up to the All-knowing and trust the fact of that, means not looking to my own will or knowledge. To Look In and trust that I reflect the All-knowing means I can trust whatever idea comes with peace, calm, and clarity. Each now is filled with the presence of all-knowing, as long as I am identifying myself as the reflection of the All.

The answer came through clearly: "Go left. Go see Mel." Once I heard, "Go left," I checked if it passed the test. Did the answer make me feel peaceful, calm, and clear? Or did it bring up questions and doubts? There is no emotional charge around intuition. It feels neutral and sure. This did. To Look Out meant taking action on the idea. I trusted the guidance and turned left.

Forty minutes later, Mel and I got settled on the couch with our hot drinks for a good talk. We'd just found our conversational rhythm, filled with laughter and pinging with intuitive leaps, when Mel's housekeeper showed up.

Oh brother! I thought, *Why does this have to happen now?!*

I resented this interruption. This was my time to connect with Mel, to see her and be seen by her, to hear each other's heart as we always did. Why wasn't it going the way I thought it should? Had I misunderstood the angel-thought? Was this woman capable of thwarting what I thought was the divine plan for me today? Clearly, I was still clinging to the ego's outline for the way the day was *supposed* to go, and I needed to let go.

Then I looked up at the woman. We'll call her Mary. I was a little taken aback. Mary looked down and said something very softly, as if she wished she were invisible and we wouldn't notice her or the heavy sadness. She was obviously depressed. My heart went out to her, and in an instant of feeling her emotional state, I felt compassion. I wanted Mary to feel safe.

I looked at her long enough to gently draw her gaze and passively enough not to frighten her off, as if looking at a skittish shelter animal who doesn't trust people. Mary and I connected in a way you sometimes do even before words are spoken. In that space between words, I felt her trust me, and then she met my gaze for just

a moment, long enough to engage. I was led by my heart — asked
a few questions to know more about who she was — and almost
immediately, she shared intimate issues of her life. Mary said she felt
unloved, purposeless, out of control, worthless. She loved a man more
than she ever had — but was in a push-pull relationship with him that
left her feeling alone and scared. She felt bereft of worth, like she had
nothing to offer.

Then Mary mentioned suicide. I knew what that felt like from a past
experience and recalled the truth that pulled me out of that darkness.
This got my attention more focused on seeing who she was beyond the
story. I knew she had a choice and would find her way out of all this by
understanding not her *boyfriend's* love but *God's* love for her.

We got into a deep conversation about Looking Up, who God is,
and how much He loves us. I shared the idea that when you solidify
your relationship with divine Love itself and Look In, your human
relationships naturally improve because when we Look Out, they
mirror the one true relationship we have with God. And knowing our
Source gives us more access to knowing our true selves and seeing our
value. She seemed somewhat comforted but was still discouraged.

Then I asked her, "What if you started tomorrow with love — make
an effort to connect with God and establish your relationship with
Source?"

She looked overwhelmed.

Since we are the expression of the divine, seeing our own goodness
is a step towards seeing the source of that goodness. "Try this," I
suggested. "Maybe each day, you could write down five qualities you
like about yourself, or at least would like to see yourself expressing."

I thought I saw her face soften a little. She hesitated, "I'll try. I think
I can do that." Then, on the spot, Mary came up with three qualities
she appreciated and thought she could come up with more of them if
she focused on it during the next few days.

Her manner had shifted a bit. "Don't you deserve to give yourself
that gift every day?" I asked her. "Aren't you as valuable as the plants
you water? Even more valuable! Isn't your concept of yourself and

your relationship with God just as important as a fledgling sprout in your care?"

That did it! Her face lightened and glowed. Mary left that day resolved to connect with God at the start of every day (Look Up), acknowledge her own good qualities as a creation of God (Look In), and see that she was as important as the plants she cared for (Look Out). And as she left, she said, "An *angel* has changed the course of my life today."

An angel had changed the course of my life that day too. That interchange was a gentle yet obvious reminder to me that love is of God, and that, though beautifully expressed by friends and acquaintances, love does not originate with them. God is always the source. And because of that, people can come and go, but the source of love is always present and always has an opportunity to appear in our life when we don't limit it to one place or person.

What at first felt like an interruption to my connection with Mel became a confirmation that love connects us all to exactly the right people at the right time and in the right way. The outcome far exceeded what I had imagined. All three of us were touched by the experience.

Since then, Mel heard that her housekeeper, Mary, got in touch with God each morning. As a result, Mary feels more sure of who she is, and her appreciation of her own goodness is growing.

Helping an unhappy woman learn how to connect with God a little better made me feel loved and needed, too, and I felt that I was doing His will. That morning my desire had been to serve and fulfill divine purpose — to do the best thing I could — and I had listened to and followed God's plan. As it turned out, what may have looked like my feeling of compassion for someone else was also a sign of God loving me in a wonderful way. God opens a path for us to walk on that meets the needs of others and in the process, our needs are met too. We have the choice whether or not we step onto the path we are shown by the intuitions and inspiration that come to us. When we show up in a service mindset, ready to give to others, willing to be used by Life, the opportunities to serve appear.

EXERCISE: *Start a Love Journal*

I would love to invite you to take up the practice each day that I suggested to Mary. Each morning when you wake up, write down five qualities you like, or dare I say, love about yourself. Perhaps keep this list in your very own love journal dedicated just to your growing sense of self-appreciation. One of the first exercises I do with my clients is what we affectionately call "The List of 100," where I ask them to write a list of one hundred things they love about themselves. Most get stuck around ten or fifteen positive qualities, yet have no hesitation — or shortage — when it comes to listing negative things they feel about themselves. But there's a trick. Once you get stuck coming up with good qualities, write the negative ones in a separate place and then reverse them. So if you don't like that you're selfish, add generous to your list. The list then becomes aspirational, and this more accurate vision of who you are, held in thought, will bring these qualities into expression. Not only does this exercise very quickly help you realize how much you speak negatively to yourself, it will help train you to reverse the lie and start claiming the truth. Remember, what we focus on expands, and we want to be *for* the good qualities as opposed to *against* the negative qualities.

# CHAPTER 5

Listen, Follow, and Act

*By giving earnest heed to these spiritual guides they tarry
with us, and we entertain "angels unawares."*
— Mary Baker Eddy

I grew up in Cohasset, halfway between Boston and Cape Cod in Massachusetts. We lived on the ocean so I never felt the need to fight traffic and head south to the Cape. But after marriage and our move to the West Coast, the opportunity to stay on the Cape in my husband's family home a few times a year became a favorite break, a chance to reconnect with my New England roots and the quaint seaside communities of my youth.

The Cape house faced west, so we spent evenings hanging out on the deck, feet up on the rail, watching the sunset over Oyster Harbor's West Bay dotted with sailboats, listening to the air-horn blasts of tall-masted sailboats signaling the drawbridge keeper to raise the bridge one last time before darkness fell.

My mom, daughter Makenna, and I had been at the house for a few days. My husband J. and son Kelemn would arrive the next day. Makenna was out sailing. Mom and I donned our suits and headed out for a swim. I walked to the end of the dock for a quick-plunge approach, while Mom opted for the gradual inching-in approach from the beach. Anticipating the chill of early summer water, I stood there debating with myself about which was worse. Mummy got into the water before I did. I stood on the dock, not jumping in. Very uncharacteristic of me. Once I made up my mind to go off the end of the dock, it was usually three, two, one, jump. This time was different, as though a hand held me back.

I stepped down a rung on the ladder and felt the water with my toe. I never did this! It was almost a cardinal rule for me to not test the temperature when diving off the dock. Better to commit and go for it. The water was pretty warm. But I went back up the ladder, still not sure what all the delay was about. I wanted to go swimming. Why was this happening? I was being guided without knowing it, or as some say, "entertaining angels unawares."

Mummy squealed with delight, little high-pitched sounds that escape unbidden when submerging in cold water. That happened a few times. I was focused on diving in. Good for Mummy; she dunked before I did.

I was just about to dive — my hands raised and arcing toward the water — when there was another sound from my mom, the same as before. This time an alarm went off in my head. I snapped to attention. I don't know how to describe it other than to say, I knew something was wrong, even though the squeals sounded playful and happy as they had before.

I turned to see my mom struggling in two feet of water right near the beach. Had she lost her balance walking into the water? It was impossible to tell.

"Are you okay?"

No answer.

She was on her back, arms flailing, panicking, and going under! It wasn't deep enough for her to get her feet under her, and she didn't seem to have enough body control to roll over to get her hands down. She was gasping for air, but choking on salt water. I bolted down the dock, down the stairs into the shallows, leaping the divide of water between us. All I could do was scoop her body weight onto my knees to lift her chest and head above the waterline. She was delirious and shaken, but she could breathe. With a few gulps of air and coughing up seawater, her panic subsided. Her eyes focused again.

If I had dived off the end of the dock, there's no way I would have been able to save my mom. Something stopped me from diving in. A force bigger than my conscious awareness halted my normal routine and kept my mom safe. I trust these moments are not a coincidence. I see so much evidence of this governing force, this law of good, operating. When we choose to be governed by the law of good, it guides us even when we're not focused on it.

Because I am tuned in and practiced at Looking Up, Looking In, and Looking Out as my constant rhythm, I don't resist the little nudges that guide me. I yield to angels even when not doing it consciously. We can all be guided to more good, safety, and harmony. We can all make this our practice.

Feel confident that what you accept into thought as true about yourself must become your experience.

Your daily practice brings your life into alignment with the spiritual laws that govern. Know God and know your true self. Align thought with what is true and not the illusion of externals. Feel confident that what you accept into thought as true about yourself must become your experience. This is your daily practice. Disciplining yourself to notice where you place your attention and focus is what will change your life for the better. It is a living practice, always taking place and always available as spiritual power.

The whole next section will guide you to design your own daily practice. But for now, you must make a choice that life is *for* you, not *against* you, and commit to a practice that brings you into alignment with this law of good. We either accept it and practice it, or we doubt it and postpone the possibility of a life expanded to its fullest.

✳ CHAPTER 6 ✳

Spiritual Warrior Training — Daily Practice

My prayer, some daily good to do
To Thine, for Thee;
An offering pure of Love, whereto
God leadeth me.
— Mary Baker Eddy

A daily spiritual practice changed my life, and it can do the same for you. I can't emphasize this enough. The very premise of our thinking is forged by our daily habits of thought. It has been well documented that an individual's mental state plays a role in their health, either positively or negatively. For instance, our level of stress — or more accurately, our response to it — directly impacts our mental and physical health. When we establish a spiritual mindset each day based on the fact that our consciousness is a reflection of divine Mind, and we choose our response to thoughts that float by, we proactively govern our experience. Remember, human consciousness equals human experience. If we don't establish the basis of our mindset each day, the world is doing it for us, and instead of being proactive in our response to the world, we are in a constant state of reaction to it. In this chapter, I'll give you a chart to work with to design your own daily practice, then I'll give you all the reasoning behind it. But let's cut to the chase and give you the goods up front. This chart is designed for you to start with who you want to *be* and let that drive what you want to *do* in your daily practice to achieve that way of being. Being drives doing.

In the chart below ask yourself each question from the perspective of Look Up, Look In, Look Out. Here are the full questions you see abbreviated in the chart below:

- Who would You have me be?

- What would You have me know?

- What would You have me see?

- What would You have me do?

- Where would You have me go?

- What would You have me say and to whom?

By answering these questions from these three perspectives, you'll establish your practice on the 3 Essential Elements, your relationship with the divine, the self, and others.

- **Look Up** to a power larger than self.

- **Look In** to your highest self, and recognize that you are not separate but at one with the divine source of your being. You include all that the divine is. As an example, Jesus stated it this way, "I and my Father are one."

- **Look Out** to act as your highest self with others and to see others in their highest self. Be your truest self with others and create the space for others to be their truest self with you.

By filling in the chart, you will identify elements you want to include in your Practice.

Design the Elements of Your Daily Spiritual Practice

Use the example below as a jumping off point. There's a blank chart at the end of the chapter for you to fill in on your own.

	LOOK UP	LOOK IN	LOOK OUT
Who would you have me Be? What would you have me Know and See? (What qualities do I express while my focus is up, in, out? What kind of person do I want to be?)	Be clear on who God is, understand that I am at one with God, release control, receive all good. (Reverent, humble, quiet, patient, grateful . . .)	See and love myself as the pure reflection of the divine. Be clear that I can of my own self do nothing. (Alert, humble, expectant, loving . . .)	Be the reflection of God. Be in a service mindset. (Unselfed, giving, kind, humble, generous, brave, patient, of service, perceptive, intuitive . . .)
What would you have me Do? (What can I do to bring out those qualities while my intention is up, in, and out?)	Know absolute God. Affirm true Ego. Listen to God. (Pray, be still, and know. Review lessons. Read, journal, lean on God, listen, see glory, push beyond limits . . .)	See my wholeness. See Godlike-self, not personality. Love who I am. (Journal, focus on good, write affirmations, eat well, exercise, discipline thought . . .)	Be in service to Love. Give. Listen and follow. (Practice listening each morning before rising. Bravely follow God's voice and speak truth. Listen to hearts not words . . .)
Where would you have me Go? (Where would I go as I'm guided by God, my highest self, being in service to others?)	Go where I feel the power of God, that gets me beyond self. (Go into nature. Be around animals, art, music, design, style. Dance, sing, eat good food . . .)	Be still in a favorite place and spend time alone. (Go to the ocean, overlook, home, mountain, walk/run first thing, explore new, challenge comfort . . .)	Listen to God's guidance and be obedient in following. (Show up to inspire others. Offer to help, give, serve, drive, support . . .)

	LOOK UP	LOOK IN	LOOK OUT
What would you have me Say and to Whom? (What will I say and to whom, when I'm focused up, in, out?	Talk to God. Talk about God. (Tell stories of healing. Express gratitude. Inspire with words, attitude, and serenity at the store, on the street, in family . . .)	Be kind and truthful to yourself. Speak only truth to and about yourself and others. (Be disciplined about self-talk, self-view, and be honest . . .)	Speak from the heart. (Be brave with kind words and deeds to all I know and don't yet know. Vow to restrain pen and tongue. Be the calm for others . . .)

The first question is "Who would you have me be?" You'll answer that one question from three perspectives — Up, the divine; In, yourself; and Out, others. Who does God want you to be, and who do you want to be in relationship with the divine? Who do you want to be in relationship with yourself? Who do you want to be in relationship with others?

In each case, ask yourself, what activity would bring out that way of being? That's what you'd write in the box. If in relationship to the divine, I want to be humble and still, what activity could I choose that would call those qualities out in me? Perhaps meditation would demand humility and stillness of me, so I would incorporate time for mediation in my practice. Or perhaps I want to be disciplined, so establishing a set time for meditation and prayer might be part of my commitment so that I'm expressing discipline by following that schedule.

Then I'd ask the same questions based on my relationship with myself. Who do I want to be for me? I want to be kind to myself and love myself. What could I do that would demonstrate that in my daily practice? Perhaps writing out affirmations of my good qualities, taking time to take a longer shower or to pick out an outfit might be part of my practice, running every day so I feel energized, or making my bed so I feel accomplished. These may seem like small commitments, but because we build them into our consistent daily practice, they are powerful tools for shaping who we are and how we show up for ourselves and others.

Now, follow the same thought process to complete each row and column in the chart and discover the elements of your own Daily Spiritual Practice to Look Up, Look In, and Look Out. Designing your practice is an ongoing process. You get to revisit this as often as you need to. If you notice the practice is not inspiring you or it's feeling rote, it may be time to switch things up and find a new activity that prompts a particular way of being. Another hint that you need to revisit your practice is when you feel no joy in it — when it's running you instead of reflecting your heart's desire. Let your practice transform as you do. See it as a fluid expression of your heart's desire to see yourself fully, as God sees you. I'll go into more of the reasoning shortly, but better to dive in and try it for yourself.

Let who you want to BE drive what you DO during your Daily Spiritual Practice (what you know, what you see, what you do, where you go, what you say, and to whom). Remember it's being, doing, having (not having, doing, being).

What are some examples of "being" in the Up-In-Out Way?

Be grateful, humble, reverent, receptive, consistent, disciplined, confirming, understanding, unselfed, at one, introspective, strong, peaceful, precise, perceptive, exact, thorough, divine, joyful, childlike, fluid, graceful, appreciative, loving, blessed, etc. What ways of being will you focus on?

What are some ways of "doing" in the Up-In-Out Way?

Read, listen, move, meditate, sit in silence, exercise, connect to nature/animals, play music, create art, journal, write treatments, speak I Am statements, state affirmations, hike, walk animals, stand still, etc.

What ways of "doing" do you recognize in your life?

As you can see from the worksheet, your daily spiritual practice includes three essential elements: your relationship with the divine, your relationship with yourself, and your relationship with everything that seems to be outside of yourself, including others and the world. You also might notice that these three relationships reflect the structure, Look Up, Look In, Look Out. And in the chart you followed Look Up, Look In, Look Out to choose which activities you want to include in your daily practice. It's a daily spiritual practice seen through the Up-In-Out lens. The Up-In-Out approach is going to apply to every aspect of who you are, how you see your source, yourself, and how you see others, and who you choose to be, know, see, do, and say with them and about them.

What is a daily spiritual practice going to give you? Or better yet, who will you become as a result of it? Be aware that it's not what you're going to *get from it*. It's *who you're going to be in it*. That's the whole point.

Start with "Why?" Why do you want a Daily Spiritual Practice?

What's your why? Why is it important for *you* to commit to a daily practice?

In Simon Sinek's book *Start with Why*, he explains that successful companies go from why to how to what, not the other way around. He wrote, "People don't buy what you do. They buy why you do it." With daily practice we go from who to how to what, which is all bolstered by why. If we are clear about why we are doing a daily practice, we will continue doing it without needing to convince ourselves each morning that it's what we want to do. We'll want to do it because of who we want to be, or more accurately, because we want to express who we already are. Ultimately, our practice is based on who we are and is part of the natural expression of our being.

Our daily practice will drive us to discover what's right for us, and our practice will become a natural extension of our whole true self. Then it won't be dependent on human will, it will be the sacred time and space of at-one-ment where we feel filled up with our natural divinity. A daily practice carries us throughout the day, blessing not only our experience, but the experience of all with whom we come in contact.

Some of you might say, "I have a daily practice to stay on top of my day or to stay aligned with my higher power when things get tough." But let's go even deeper! In the spirit of *Seven Levels Deep*, courtesy of Dean Graziosi and Joe Stump, why is *that* important to us? Keep asking, "Why?" until we get to a place where we can't find another, deeper answer. Knowing our "Why" helps us stay committed to the practice.

How do I do a daily practice? We get to doing through being.

Don't start with *doing*. Start with *being* — who we are, and who we're being. The world advocates and embodies a flawed model: Go do stuff, so you can get more and have more stuff, and then with all that *stuff*, be happy. It's flawed because it's backwards.

How many times have we heard the story of the gazillionaire who is miserable? They have all the stuff in the world, and yet they feel empty and unfulfilled. That's because they don't know who they are or how to be happy within themselves. The reverse is actually true. Know who you are, be who you are, be content within yourself, and you will see contentment in all you do because you *are* contentment; you are not seeking contentment outside of yourself.

When you are water, you can take the shape of any container and still be water. You are not an empty vessel trying to be filled up from the outside. Your substance is who you are, and who you are determines your shape, the outward expression of you. Not the other way around. Don't look outside of yourself to get filled up. Look within to know you are already full. Thus the order of thinking in your daily practice: Source, you, other(s).

What do I include? Identify elements you want to include in your Practice.

What do I need to *do* in my practice? Do I read? Do I go walking in nature? Do I sit still? What activities are involved?

There are many ways to decide what will be included in your daily spiritual practice, which follows the Look Up, Look In, Look Out model. It's your practice, nobody else's. The important thing to remember is that you can always change it, refresh it, let it morph as you morph. It serves you and your well-being. It is not meant to be a burden or another item on your to-do list. It is meant to enliven and enrich you and set you up for your day.

Once you design the elements of your daily practice, think carefully about when you will do this. I recommend doing it first thing, starting even before you get out of bed, and definitely before you engage with technology. What are you claiming about Source and yourself before your feet touch the ground?

One of the tricks is to think of your daily practice as starting the night before with your bedtime routine. If you think of that as the start of your next day instead of just the end of the current day, it may help you enter the next day with more purpose and direction already in place. When I made that little perspective shift for myself, it was amazing what changed as a result. Knowing that I wanted to give myself more quiet time in the morning for my growing daily practice, I committed to several things: starting my evening routine earlier, setting specific intentions for the morning, claiming a restful night's sleep for myself, and getting up earlier. With that in place, getting up earlier felt natural and welcome, and I didn't start the next day with resentment for the earlier alarm. Most days I wake before my alarm. You might try starting your day the night before and see what shifts for you.

Identify the activities that will scaffold you into the ways of being that are important to you. "Habit stack" (thank you James Clear), which traditionally means stacking a new habit on top of an established one. For example, every time you go through the doorway, you do three squats to add more exercise to your day. This is a little different take on it. Attach a desired way of being to an activity. In other words, pick an activity that prompts you into a way of being. If you want to be more disciplined, you might choose to run every morning in order to let the habit pull you into being more disciplined.

Examples of Spiritual Habit Stacking — the Physical-Spiritual stack or Do-Be stack:

- You wake up every day. So what habit of thought could you add to that moment? When you wake up, identify yourself spiritually, pray and listen to God, list what you're grateful for, go through daily prayers, commit to loving yourself and others, etc.

- You get out of bed every day. So what habit of thought could that action prompt for you? Each time you get out of bed, express your desire to serve God and be an instrument for peace. (My feet don't touch the floor until I'm in a service mindset, available to do God's work. I ask myself, "Am I willing to do whatever intuition guides me to without argument? Am I putting God first? Am I serving God and putting self aside?")

- You exercise. During that time, get in the habit of seeing and acknowledging who you're being during that time: disciplined, unlimited, selfless, free, communing with nature, being in the present, flexible, strong, etc.

You get the idea . . . build in activities that prompt ways of being to Look Up, Look In, and Look Out!

Determine a schedule for your practice and commit to it.

Write down your commitment to yourself and post it in a place where you'll see it every day. Remembering your "why" will help you stay consistent.

Once our thought is established for the day with our daily spiritual practice, we have the opportunity to choose — choose to utilize and see with spiritual sense instead of material sense throughout the day.

Your daily habits of declaration and the standpoint from which you operate make all the difference in what you see evidenced in your life — what shows up in your life. You have the choice to claim Love instead of fear as the basis of life. As Einstein said, "There are only two ways to live your life. One is as though nothing is a miracle. The other is as though everything is a miracle." You get to decide and your choice will determine your experience. Choose that everything is a miracle, and your life will be a miracle. Choose that Love is governing, and fear will dissipate from your life. It's proportionate. The more you claim Love, the less you will claim fear. The more you accept the power of Love as governing, the more you will see evidence of Love governing. Right where fear shows up, there's a possibility of seeing the reality of Love. Choose Love.

	LOOK UP	LOOK IN	LOOK OUT
Who would you have me Be? (What qualities do I express while my focus is up, in, out? What kind of person do I want to be?)			
What would you have me Know? (What qualities do I express while my focus is up, in, out? What do I want to know?)			
What would you have me See? (What qualities do I express while my focus is up, in, out? What do I want to see?)			
What would you have me Do? (What can I do to bring out those qualities while my intention is up, in, and out?)			
Where would you have me Go? (Where would I go as I'm guided by God, my highest self, being in service to others?)			
What would you have me Say and to Whom? (What will I say and to whom, when I'm focused up, in, out?			

✦ ✦ ✦ PART 2 ✦ ✦ ✦

Understanding the Source

There is one Source. Good is All. All is Good. Nothing flows from another source. Therefore, when we understand the allness of one Source, our life gets a whole lot simpler.

If I stand on a rock in the middle of a rushing river, I am not affected by the current. The rock is a fixed and stable place from which to operate. But if I am in the rushing river and am clamoring to get back on the rock, I will feel the effect of all the currents and forces of the water.

God always sees us on the rock. That's who we are and how we were made. Where I see myself and identify myself will shift my experience. If I know I am tributary only to one Source, God, good, I feel empowered, steady, abundant, free. If I think I'm subject to all the currents of mortal thought, I feel tumbled and tossed by the mortal experience and its expressed laws based on matter. I have the choice to be governed by the understanding of the allness and all-power of good or the belief that the mortal sense of things has power. That choice will govern my experience. That choice will give me either freedom or limitation. Understanding the allness of God — and myself as an expression of God — is paramount to governing my experience.

We can't know our true self without knowing the Source from which we came. So in this section, we look at the power of Source and how understanding Source and ourselves in alignment with Source has a profound effect on our life.

CHAPTER 7

Perfection Is the State of Being

All is infinite Mind and its infinite manifestation,
for God is All-in-all.
— Mary Baker Eddy

"**N**o words!" is all I could say. So using words to describe this event is less than ideal. It opened a door in consciousness, confirmed a knowing and confidence inside, and explained so much of the otherness I'd always felt. The most important point to remember when you read this is that this experience is not unique to me; everyone has the same capacity to feel connected or at one with the all-knowing Mind, to have no doubt or fear, to feel completely at one with the divine and enveloped in Love.

Some experiences are beyond words and descriptions. I've had many of these experiences, but the most profound one that truly changed my life happened when I was eighteen. I want to describe the conditions leading up to it because you may see patterns that are important for you that only you can discern.

I was physically exhausted but spiritually enlivened. I'd just completed my freshman year of college final exams. The intensity of focus and lack of sleep required for finals was a spiritual experience, meaning, it prompted me to rely on a power larger than my ego and intellect. The whole process challenged me to go higher, Look Up to the all-power of God, Look In and claim intelligence and strength as a reflection of the divine, and then Look Out to demonstrate that truth in doing and achieving.

Right afterwards, I drove twenty-four hours nonstop to volunteer as an usher at a church International Youth Meeting (IYM) in Boston.

It was a gathering of inspirational leaders from around the world, speaking to tens of thousands of students. The three days were filled with inspiration that left me spiritually primed and in a place of humility and expression that was purely aligned.

I was also in a relationship. Scott and I started dating halfway through my freshman year. We shared a mutual desire to understand God, Spirit, Truth more than physical affection. That was there too, but it didn't feel as interesting or important as the thought-pinging spiritual expansion we experienced together. We shared regular bursts of insight. This was my bliss. Always has been. After finals, he came with me across the country to attend the IYM and stayed with us at my mom's house in rural New England.

After three very full days of meetings filled with inspiration, we went for a walk under the summer night sky in the flat neighborhood near my mom's. Our conversation about UFOs and higher intelligence, prompted somewhat by the movie we'd just seen about alien invasion, got interesting.

"If a UFO landed in front of us right now, would you go?" He walked faster as he asked, excited by the prospect.

"Absolutely! If they know how to get here, they'd know how to bring me back." Without a shred of doubt, this solid conviction opened something in me. I kept hearing a phrase in my head — *expanding consciousness*. Was it a line I'd heard in the movie? I wasn't sure, but the phrase would almost haunt me later as a reverberation of pure truth.

I had the choice to stay or go: stay on this plane and in this body or not.

The next few blocks of our walk are a bit of a blur. I can't tell you what we talked about, but I remember that words became very, very heavy and cumbersome. I remember feeling my thinking speed up — ideas came without words, going so fast that there was no time to decide if I should think them — ideas of allness, higher intelligence, identity beyond body — vast and infinite ideas. They just . . . were.

Every time Scott said something, I felt annoyed, as though I was in the high-speed lane on a five lane freeway, and he was in the breakdown lane reaching out to grab my hand. It wasn't possible. Every word out of his mouth was a grappling hook hurled at me, digging in, slowing me down, and lurching me to a stop. Thought raced. I was filled with knowing, feeling, a sense of God's allness and goodness, a sense of well-being and bursting excitement and contentment. This knowing did not take the form of words, but his words coming at me forced me to hear and think in words. I didn't want to slow down to listen or contemplate sluggish words. I couldn't bear it. No matter what he said, all I could say was, "No words!" in increasingly strident tones.

We walked in silence the rest of the way around the block, returned to my mom's shingled split-level ranch on Country Way, and Scott, I'm sure a bit frustrated with my state, went left, down the half flight to the guest room, while I, oblivious of my surroundings, went up the half flight to the kitchen for some orange juice.

The feelings of inspiration and awe were overwhelming. You know when you watch the Olympics or a Hallmark commercial and tears well up and the emotion overtakes you? It was like that on steroids. I kept catching my breath as awe-inspired tears flowed. The feeling didn't subside; it kept growing stronger — more heightened and more encompassing — my heart bursting with awe and wonder and expansion.

My body felt very energized as I stood there with the glass of juice in hand, staring at the light switch, and I heard a voice or a thought in my head.

"Put down the glass."

I put the glass down. I put my hands on the counter.

I kept hearing (well, it was more like knowing) commands. "Close your eyes." As I stood in front of the counter, my hands drifted down and palms rested on the cool Formica, it was as if a force were moving me. I felt myself lean back, which drew my hands to the edge of the counter. I thought I would fall back. There was no impulse to stop the motion. Instead of falling, I felt myself go up. Whether I levitated at that point, I don't know. All I can share is what it felt like.

So much was happening at once: breathing choppy, tears streaming, thoughts racing beyond words, knowing the truth of ideas flowing in, awareness of the counter slipping away from the end of my fingers, fear of falling back, questioning why I didn't fall, yielding to the moment, not understanding the moment, judging and not judging, awareness of spiritual and physical aspects of me, being obedient to thoughts coming in, allowing the ideas to just be without question, observing . . . so much all at once, and a desire and openness for more.

There were no questions about why this was happening — only the idea, "This is so cool!" over and over again. There was a whole component of my mental and spiritual state that was happening simultaneously. I was hyper-aware that ideas were racing through consciousness and going so fast that it was impossible to think in terms of specific words or even specific thoughts. Ideas presented themselves and just "were." I simply "knew" things that I needed to know in the moment, like I was being given direction or understanding that filled each instant. There was no sense of time or space or doubt. This was a place of pure knowing, pure bliss, pure consciousness — all that is — present in the moment, the now.

While this state of thought was present, there was another part of me that was aware of my body, like there was a physical body, me, and a spiritual body, me. I was modulating back and forth between them in my awareness. I was losing the feeling in my body. It felt important to be aware of this, although I could not say why. And it's occurring to me as I write this to note that I wasn't aware of my surroundings. The physical environment wasn't a consideration. Like the experience was suspended, devoid of time and space. It was all ideas.

Ideas just were. You know the way an idea occurs to us and then we accept it or reject it? In this case, there was no decision or choice. They simply existed. Ideas instantaneously manifested as my present reality, as what was happening for me. Here's an example.

In an instant, a lesson from a college class came to mind. We were asked to close our eyes and think of someone in the class.

"What did you all think about?" the teacher, Alan, asked us.

We all rattled off physical attributes and descriptors.

"Now think of the same person using nothing outward or physical; think about their spiritual qualities," he guided. The point was an obvious one.

"Now do the same thing with a city," Alan said.

I'd been to Paris as a child and thought of the Eiffel Tower and Arc de Triomphe.

And again came the gentle guidance, "Do it in terms of qualities."

This was followed by a whole discussion about thought travel and why it would be possible since cities were spiritual ideas, reflective of spiritual qualities, and not solid places at all. Of course *thought-travel* was possible from that standpoint. Then the question became, what got in the way of experiencing it?

This whole discussion and conclusion that thought-travel was a real possibility appeared in consciousness for me as a singular idea. And in the same space I challenged the idea, "Prove it!"

I'm describing this linearly, but it was all at once. The same instant, I found myself standing in Paris on the Champs Élysées, staring at the Arc de Triomphe, people rushing past speaking French in echoes of reality. And as soon as I actually felt myself there and knew I wasn't dreaming, I was back with a kind of I-told-you-so feeling pushing in on my awareness.

There was no time, no fear, no limitation. The next instant I was above my body in the kitchen, looking down at myself standing there. Oddly, this wasn't a surprise. It seemed the most natural thing. Then, again an idea was present. It was a quote from *Science and Health*: "The astronomer will no longer look up to the stars, — he will look out from them upon the universe; and the florist will find his flower before its seed." Like before, my experience mirrored the idea.

An other-worldly force pulled me up and out beyond the house, up into darkness in an instant, with the Earth fading fast into the vast forever of space. I was out among the stars, experiencing and proving the prophetic phrase that had presented itself as truth. I looked out from the stars instead of up to them. And again, as soon as I was aware this was real, the process reversed. I went back down to Earth and into the kitchen faster than going up into space.

Words completely pale in describing the all-encompassing awe. It was like being hard-wired to God. Whatever God was, I was. Whatever God thought, I thought. Whatever God knew, I knew. But this feeling could not be contained in words. I just knew this was reality. I knew this was all there is. I knew anything and everything could be healed, was possible, normal, obvious. I knew all was one. There is no separation. There is no space — literally — but also no space between an idea and its expression. Ideas were instantaneously known instead of being thought. Everything flowed. There was no time or space or fear. Only love. Pure love. Instantaneous and infinite love. All.

*And in the same instant, I was aware
of a choice. Stay or go.*

"This is so cool!" didn't come in words. It was a feeling, an overwhelming desire to share what I was experiencing, to share the feeling of awe and knowing and clarity, to share the certainty of what was so clear in that moment, what was true and real. Communication came as feelings rather than thoughts. The feeling was "This is so cool!" while tears still streamed. The physical body, me, and the spiritual body, me, had progressed almost completely to the spiritual side. I'd lost all the feeling in my body except for my feet, as if my feet contained the weight of my whole body.

The idea appeared, again more as a knowing or certainty than as a thought, "If you lose the feeling in your feet, you will not go back to your body." There was no question of this. And in the same instant, I was aware of a choice. Stay or go. It was a clearly defined point of decision. There was no impending feeling or judgment that came with the idea — just a *knowing* that I had the choice to stay or go: stay on this plane and in this body or not.

There was no sense of danger or loss, just overwhelming awe, so overflowing. It was coupled with a desire to share it, and simultaneously, an awareness of my brother Hal and of Scott. It was a present sense of them, a feeling of them more than a thought of them. It was as though the outpouring of awe needed a place to land, and there was a desire to share this knowing, share the experience of awe with them.

"I want to share this! I want to share this! This is so cool!" There were no words, but the feeling was beyond containment, bursting out of my being, a fire burning everything in its path. All-consuming knowing presented itself. Knowing filled my being with the resonance of Truth. "Healing is possible." "This allness is all that really is." "Everything else is the illusion of limits." "Healing is possible."

This idea about healing was powerfully present. There was no time or space or fear or doubt present. There were no limits or specific thoughts. There were no outlines in consciousness. The feeling of all-encompassing Love and Peace, Knowing and Allness were the expanse of my being.

With this understanding of reality, the problems of three dimensions seemed easily overcome and in essence, healed by true reality. If what I knew was true became all of my conscious awareness, then there was no room in there for the awareness of a problem. Healing was the natural result of this understanding.

It was very clear what I wanted and was being called to do. I knew I was meant to share what I'd been given, this glimpse into the All. The fact of it all. The reality of Love. The power of God. There was no doubt or fear or hesitation. There were no questions. There were no concrete thoughts. Ideas just were. Perfection is a state of being and expanding consciousness.

In fact, that phrase was something that stayed with me for months, years, and continues as a current beacon. I experienced the ever-expanding consciousness of perfect being. If I had to sum up this experience in one phrase, that would come close — expanding consciousness.

The choice was clear. Stay. Share this knowing. Remind people. This potential for awareness is present inside each of us. We all have access to it. We can all experience this expanding consciousness and find healing. We can all feel at one with Allness and limitless freedom. It is just beyond the veil of acceptance. If people only knew how close it is. Believe and so it is. Understand and be. We are the expression of

All. There was no time. The feeling of knowing all, understanding all, was my very identity.

Once I chose to stay, the process of the spiritual-body me and physical-body me started to reverse itself. The spiritual-body me was in now-awareness with no limits, time, space, fear, doubt. And the physical-body me was in time and space awareness of my surroundings. I started to get the feeling back in my body, the pins and needles of a limb waking up that'd fallen asleep. I had no idea how much time had elapsed. The body-thing felt strange — off, limiting, restrictive, archaic, ancient — something that we had long-since outgrown. After being hard-wired to God and then forced to think and act as a mortal with limits was like being a lightsaber asked to act like a squirt gun.

Slowly . . . slowly . . . this engine of knowing, which was revved higher than sound could register, consciously downshifted, unselfishly transitioned, like the master professor of quantum physics slowing down to explain to a first grader. The engine of infinite knowing slowed its gears to a pace of ancient comprehension. The All-knowing understood that the present circumstances of time and space demanded translation. A story is told, a parable perhaps, with secrets buried deep inside for those able to discern the true meaning. The world of unlimited and infinite, all-knowing Spirit communicating with thought hemmed in by thinking and reasoning and the structure of matter, time, and limits felt like a gear spinning at a blinding pace made to sync with a gear just starting to spin. The need was to s – l – o – w d – o – w – n.

The All-knowing is perceptible in flashes to the limited thought. It's like when you get a flash of the mountain when the clouds briefly lift, and when they descend again, you keep the image of the mountain distinctly in thought, despite the fact that all you see is clouds. You see the clouds, but you know the reality of the mountain.

Can we look through a finite lens to perceive infinity? Impossible. To see infinity on the head of a pin is materially impossible, but every attempt is worthy and full of glory. Just because the task seems impossible to a limited sense of reality, doesn't mean we shouldn't keep reaching. We must focus on what we can do, not on what we can't. We must look for and focus on the pinpricks of light in the vast forever of darkness as the light sparks hope and a yearning for further glimpses of the infinite reality. It's when time and space part for an instant and the glory of it all leaves an impression on thought here and now, leaving you with a certainty without an explanation.

Once the body became my awareness again, I was conscious of standing in the kitchen. I had no idea how much time had passed and whether I was actually there or not. Was I alive? Was I experiencing reality in time and space? It all felt foreign, otherworldly, transformed, new and old. I placed my palms on the wall in front of me, then on the counter. Paused to feel the cool of the paint on the wall and the smooth, cool Formica, let it seep into me as substance, solid, an idea in form. I had no sense of identity in my body. I was still the spiritual-body me; only now I was being forced to reconcile this odd sensation of matter and limits, and light and dark.

I needed confirmation that I existed on this plane. Afraid to use my voice for fear of it not working, I cracked out a wimpy, "Scott?" I called out again with growing urgency, each new inquiry working its way up to a crescendo as I descended the stairs to the basement where Scott was sleeping. I was still completely unaware of time, but clearly I'd woken him. He sat up. I sandwiched his hand with both of mine, almost in desperation. I needed confirmation that he was there, that I was there, that we existed in the same time and space. Everything was untethered, floating, unmoored in the space around me. My very existence uncertain.

The next day we went to the beach. If it hadn't been for Scott asking me a zillion questions, forcing me to wrap words around a wordless experience, I'm not sure how much of this I could have just told you. Scott and I shared a love of Spirit and Truth, and our whole relationship was anchored in this exploration. He was the perfect scabbard to the sword of Truth that sliced open reality. How to contain it? How to keep it from cutting me out of this place of humanness. With questions, he guided my expression into words.

It took several months to feel grounded in this reality. I didn't care about anything to do with 3-D existence. Why brush teeth or get dressed or talk? It was all too slow. It all felt superficial and synthetic. I wanted to run up and grab people by the shoulders and shake them, "Don't you get it?! This isn't real!"

I was in a constant state of yearning to dwell in the place I'd seen and known and felt. What remained was a deep knowing of this reality and the stark contrast with what we are shown and told to believe is real.

A few days after it happened, after Scott had left, I started to feel thoughts racing again, just like they had when we walked around the block. I felt that same inspiration and welling up inside. I heard a voice or felt prompted to go to my room and start writing. I wrote what I heard; I took dictation. All the details of the experience came flowing out on paper. Elements that hadn't even come out on the beach that day, surfaced. The words filled pages and pages of a yellow legal pad, which I saved for years, noting its location in each new living situation, across the country and back. And then somewhere, in some move, when I wasn't keeping track, it went missing. I have to trust that when it's right for me to see it again, it will turn up.

There have been many other instances when "that feeling" has come over me and because of being around people or causing others concern, I've shut it down. But the shift in me that occurred that night has remained: the knowing, the certainty, the clarity of what's true. It opened up a portal in me which I believe is a part of all of us. A place available for anyone who desires to access it. A place of fully knowing the present and all truth contained in this now, including the past and the future, not in a linear sense, but in a present-now, infinite-now sense, which includes the future and the past.

I was so certain of the Truth and the possibility of healing that it was increasingly difficult to reconcile this illusion with what I now knew for sure. Small comfort from Einstein calling this an illusion albeit a very persistent one. Days stretched into months, frustration lessened, and I acquiesced to the day-to-day. It was impossible to reconcile, but I settled into an agreement with myself that this knowing would remain my secret, tangential reality. I never spoke of this experience beyond that day with Scott. Swore Scott to silence. I had a secret I couldn't share. I was too scared.

Then strange things started happening. I knew stuff about people that I had no business knowing. I told my friend she would meet a guy, be engaged in six months, marry in a year, and the exact housing development she would live in. One time, I met a guy at a Harvard mixer and we started chatting. After initial introductions and some conversation about what we did and where we were in life, I said something about his ex-girlfriend and some details about how hard it had been for him to move on.

He looked surprised and suspicious. "How did you know that?"

"You just told me."

He hadn't. I must have heard his thoughts so clearly inside my head that I thought he'd spoken it. He backed up quickly, assuming I was a friend of his ex and was trying to get information from him.

I knew answers without a basis of intellectual understanding, I knew people's past or futures — sometimes like watching a movie play in my head and then seeing it lived out six months later. I knew specifics about health issues and next steps before they manifested on the body. I was prompted to act on ideas and move in directions that led to more alignment, abundance, and fulfillment in my life and in service to others.

There was a certainty that would not be denied, a truth-meter against which anything could be measured. But this is not about me! *The most important point is that we all have access to this knowing inside of us. This powerful reality is true for and available to everyone.* I didn't have the courage or the language to share it right away. The world didn't talk about these things back then. These days, thanks to more people sharing their experiences, including near death experiences (NDE), the world is more open minded. (Though I would characterize my experience as a near Life experience or NLE.)

I realize only now how separate my NLE made me feel. I assumed people would think I was crazy. After all, rarely did the evidence from my external world confirm what I knew in my heart to be true. I had to give it up to survive the mundane, deny the very core of myself to make life manageable. I hid and felt ashamed that once again I was an outsider; I was different. And I wasn't comfortable being me, being different — I loved God and Spirit and from what I observed, nobody else my age did because they never talked about it or it remained hidden to me.

What I didn't realize is that everyone else, through their superficial banter, was becoming adept at social dynamics and building friendships and trust with other people. Me, not so much. I didn't trust anyone. Every time I'd attempt what I thought was an authentic conversation, it was awkward and disconnected because I only wanted to talk about deep spiritual truth, and nobody seemed remotely interested. I was met with blank stares and eye-rolls, sideways whispers, and turned backs.

Many deal with the same issues following the divorce of parents. Feeling abandoned emotionally, hiding from the shame of feeling like the family is broken, not having parents show up at functions and life's milestones. But lone-wolfing wasn't just survival, it became my way of being. Later in life, I had to learn how to ask for help or frankly, even have it occur to me that asking for help was an option.

We're all missing squares in the social-skills quilt, but mine, combined with this other-level experience became a perfect storm of social disaster. I got good at faking it — smiling, being outgoing, overscheduling myself so I didn't have time to feel anything or think about how disconnected I was. There's an element of truth to this for all of us — feeling like an outsider while watching everyone else living safe within someone's inner circle. It was like everyone else knew some secret that I wasn't privy to — how to hide in plain sight — which made me feel constantly naked. My internal fear and doubt was exposed for all to see — in my eyes, in a gesture, heard in my voice — and it demanded an elaborate dance of outgoing energy and well-placed smiles to throw them off the scent of internal terror and shame.

I hustled for acceptance and love. The divide grew between my relationship with the divine and my relationship with people. My internal world remained my secret except for those times when the force of Spirit was so powerful, it pushed up from inside and came out before I could stop it. I would speak the truth when it wasn't asked for, offer absolutes in the arena of relatives, and probably became rather annoying to anyone who had to endure what invariably sounded like a know-it-all. How horrifying it is to imagine what people must have thought. But what I now know to be true is that it's none of my business what other people think of me. That's their business, and it's between them and God. I need to align what I think of me with what God knows of me.

The lessons from this extraordinary time were not only for me — they were for others as well. Directly and profoundly, I felt hardwired to God. I knew what God knew. I experienced the All-knowing — no time, no space, no fear — only love. I beheld that place of Oneness, the instantaneity of Mind and idea. With this awareness, healing is possible. What I experienced was the reality that God is All, that Love is All. Everything unlike the All — fear, sickness, death, disease — has to be an illusion because it doesn't fit in the All. That means that what seems to be a disaster is a false or limited sense of reality.

Most important, I realized that all this knowing and consciousness — all I had experienced — could be applied to healing and sharing truth with others.

This sense of knowing, the sense of assuredness, is available to everyone! The Bible says, "the Kingdom of Heaven is within you." The Kingdom of Heaven is knowing only Love. The Kingdom of Heaven is knowing no fear. The Kingdom of Heaven is experiencing the now-ness of All-intelligence. And everyone has it within them. It's the present understanding of the All that Is. Know that.

What can you do to cultivate that understanding, to cultivate that present awareness in your day-to-day life, so that you can make the choice to lean on it? Choose to lean on that knowing. How do you get the confidence to do that? Practice. What does that look like for you? Examine your current practice or create and commit to a daily spiritual practice. It shapes your life and opens you to transformational experiences, like the story I've just shared, that lead to greater knowing and understanding.

The process outlined in the previous chapter supports you in your discovery of what your practice looks like.

- Affirm what is true in the absolute.

- Recognize and state: I am the reflection of the absolute.

- Look at what limiting beliefs come up for you that challenge the absolute. Then counter those beliefs with the absolute Truth you know.

- Then reaffirm: This law is in effect right now, and it does apply to me and my life. I can lean on it, live by it, and let it operate in my life right now. This shifts your thinking into greater and greater awareness of the All that Is.

Know that this is available to all of us. It's a part of who we are, built in. Anyone can access this deep level of understanding and operate from this place. Operate from "all is well" rather than "oh, crap, now what?" We all have the choice to claim our inherent ability to listen and to be our highest self, our divine self, our loved and guided self, the self that is the only real self — full of understanding, abundance, completeness, fulfillment, purpose, health, purity, alignment, grace, Truth, Spirit, Love.

CHAPTER 8

Nothing Separates Us from Good

Neither death, nor life, nor angels, nor principalities,
nor powers, nor things present, nor things to come,
Nor height, nor depth, nor any other creature,
shall be able to separate us from the love of God
— Romans 8

Once we understand that all the power is already inside of us, that intuition, guidance, protection, solutions, and governance are already ours to claim, we have the authority to choose this power over our circumstances. It is this choice — this ability to choose our mindset, our understanding of reality over illusion — that is our get-out of jail-free card

I was sent to Africa on a work assignment as producer for a new shortwave radio station that would be broadcasting twenty-four-hours a day around the world. A small team of us was sent to four countries in Africa — Nigeria, Kenya, Zimbabwe, and Zambia — to get to know our potential audience, find out what they were currently listening to, and learn what more they were interested in hearing. We had an enormous amount of work to accomplish in a very short time.

After Kenya, we flew to Nigeria. As soon as we landed in Nairobi, I began to feel faint, feverish, and lightheaded. We went directly from the airport into a focus-group research session with no time to do anything but drop our bags at the hotel and run.

I stood under the shade of a giant fig tree in the yard of an idyllic white church. I was interviewing a client for the research session, clutching a microphone, just conscious enough to remain standing, propped up by the tree trunk, dripping with fever, and catching myself when my knees gave out under me.

At the end of our interviews, the group stood around talking, getting to know each other. One man told the story of a woman who had recently died from malaria. He talked about the symptoms and the recurring effects of the disease. Comparing what he said to the way I felt, I became increasingly afraid I had malaria and was going to die and go home in a box.

I was scared, even though much of my preparation for this trip had focused on achieving mental and spiritual alertness through prayer. Before leaving the United States, I had called a spiritual practitioner to pray with me about issues I might have to face as a traveler — disease, unsanitary conditions, black magic and voodoo, remoteness from help, and other obstacles. I opted not to take the daily pills recommended to protect from tropical diseases. Instead, I relied on understanding, thoroughly and often, that my true protection, as well as everyone else's, comes from God.

*Could an insect biting my arm change
my relationship with God?*

Unfortunately, while I was dealing with fever and delirium, my thoughts weren't filled with such prayerful ideas. I wasn't thinking clearly, and the only thought I could muster was, "Stay conscious." KV, one of my coworkers, helped me walk back to the nearby hotel.

"KV, will you call a practitioner for me?"

"Of course, I'll get a line out to the US."

"Please just tell them what's going on and have them pray for me."

"I got a message through to the practitioner," KV said as I collapsed on the bed and passed out. My last conscious thought was someone was praying for me about how much God loves me. My friend left me to rest and met up with the rest of our group to continue the day.

BANG! BANG! BANG!

"Lisa! Lisa! Are you in there? Are you okay?" I woke from a ten-hour stupor to the booming, shaking sound of someone pounding on the door. My coworkers had missed me at dinner and wondered if I was all right. I came to with a terrible fever, barely able to lift my head. I hadn't moved one inch from where I had passed out and was lying in a puddle of sweat-soaked bedding. With the enormous amount of work to do, I didn't have time to be sick. Things didn't look good, and I was filled with fear.

"You rest. Know the practitioner's prayers are effective," KV said. "I'm right here if you need anything."

I felt calmer, knowing I was supported, and was grateful that God's love for me was not constrained by geographic distance.

This was a fork in the road. Which path would I take? My natural inclination was to pray (use my First Aid). But I was sick and scared of dying after hearing so many dire stories about malaria and yellow fever prior to the trip. It actually didn't occur to me to inquire about a medical remedy; spiritual perception of any situation had always shown me the way to go.

Since God had always been in the center of my life, I thought about how much I loved God and chose this as an opportunity to see good in the midst of the cloud of illness and fear of death. Being continents away from family and traditional comforts, I Looked Up — tuned in to God and thought about how much God loved me as my divine parent. I knew I was His/Her child and He/She would never let anything bad happen to me. And even though I couldn't talk to a spiritual practitioner right then, when I Looked In, I knew that Love was right there with me. I could feel Love and hear Love's voice. Love was all around me. And because of this, I didn't have to be afraid. I felt calmer and my mind stopped racing with fear and thoughts of death.

As a result of this shift of thought, when I Looked Out, I could expect to see health manifested, not sickness.

Then a vivid image and a question came to mind. If a mosquito were biting my arm right then, could that change the way I felt about God? Or the way God felt about me? I remember actually looking down at my arm at that moment. I laughed out loud at the ludicrous thought and asked myself, "Could an insect biting my arm change my relationship with God?" Could anything outside of me change who I was and my oneness with the divine?

The answer was obvious, "No. Of course not!" I knew that my love of and link with God could never break. So neither could my link with health, which was sourced in the divine. This alleviated my fear. I also knew that if fear is removed from a person's thoughts, complete healing of whatever is bothering that person must result. One of the pillars of this scientific system of healing is that if you remove the fear that is governing thought, you also remove the cause of the disease.

My laughter woke me up to spiritual reality. Immediately, I felt the fever break and drain from my body. I felt stronger and more stable. I sat up, absolutely confident that with this newfound, reasoned understanding, nothing could shake my certainty of God's love or my relationship with the Divine.

Over the next several weeks of the trip, I had three or four bouts of recurring symptoms. But each time, I reaffirmed what I had learned: that even if an insect bit my arm, nothing could change my oneness with God. Nothing could alter the way I felt about God or God about me. Each time, that powerful, spiritual understanding released me from the fear of disease and death. And, each time, the symptoms vanished quickly without interrupting our work. (One of the recurrences happened during an overnight bus ride from Kenya to Zimbabwe, when I had plenty of quiet time to pray and find freedom before we reached our destination.)

There were no more problems after that. It's been decades since this healing, and often since then, when faced with difficult physical illness or injury, I've Looked Out and asked myself if *any physical thing or circumstance* could change my relationship with God? And the answer has always been the same: No. And if there's ever a doubt as I Look In, I go backwards up the chain. I Look Up and affirm what I know to be true about God. Then I Look In and claim my alignment with Source and true self. And then when I Look Out, I can always expect to see God, Life, manifested and have the clarity to dismiss what the senses are telling me.

The lessons from this story are two-fold: choose and trust. When first faced with the fear of death, I chose to use the tool I was most comfortable with and had proven for myself over and over. This element speaks to the benefits of a daily practice and constant mental discipline — choosing to observe our thoughts and developing the ability to discern what is thinking chatter and what is spiritual inspiration. The awakened consciousness knows that the thinking chatter has no relationship to our true self. We are not our thoughts. Knowing this, I turned to the spiritual fact of my being instead of negative thoughts based on the physical senses. I turned the focus of my thought away from matter and toward what I knew of myself spiritually — my love for God was unchanged and unyielding, never touched by matter.

The other lesson was trust. I trusted my relationship with God, and I trusted the law of God, good, was operating even though the physical senses were telling me I had been separated from health and my very existence was in jeopardy. I trusted that the prayer of a practitioner, acknowledging my oneness with God and seeing the truth of my being, was based in the divine law that the presence of truth always pushes out the belief of error. I was barely conscious, but I trusted that acknowledging divine law was an effective method. This trust allowed me to relax and be open to good ideas. It allowed me to release a bit of the fear and feel open to inspiration and intuition. Because I was able to let go of the fear even for an instant, I was receptive to the idea that broke through the hypnotism of the moment, and I heard the question about the mosquito biting my arm.

Relying on spiritual sense instead of physical sense takes practice. And so this story highlights the importance of a daily spiritual practice, one that cultivates our confidence by cultivating our capacity to turn to Spirit.

To feel confident to choose spiritual sense in the midst of a crisis, it is really important to practice using spiritual sense when little problems come up. Doing so builds confidence that you can approach any problem from a spiritual mindset. You can remain calm and fearless and identify that whatever the problem is, it has no power to sway you from knowing your true spiritual self. You know the spiritual fact and can trust that spiritual law is governing your identity. We all have the ability to state and claim the Truth in the face of whatever problem surfaces and trust that we have the clarity to see past the 3-D evidence. This is your superpower and is inherently yours to express, not as some personal power, but as the power of God and God's law in action.

To close this chapter, I want to take our conversation one step further and then finish with a short exercise. We have looked at the difference between material and spiritual law. Now let's make the distinction between the material sense of things, which is inherently limited and finite, and the spiritual, which is inherently unlimited and infinite. This is the difference between relative perception and Reality. The relative is that place where the divine is *appearing* instead of *being*. The closer our perception is aligned with divine law, the more we see Reality instead of illusion. It's proportional.

We get to be our divine self in spite of what the world claims about us or tries to confine us to.

Spiritual law, the law of good, the law of God, is and governs Reality. What we call material law are the rules that govern our limited perception of reality based on the physical senses. Material law is actually born out of the evidence perceived by the limited physical perception of reality. For example, our perception is that train tracks come together as we look down the tracks. The physical reality is that they don't; they run parallel. It is an optical illusion caused by our limited sight that they appear to join in the distance. However, our understanding of the physical reality based on material law allows us to override the perception, and we know what is real from what is illusion.

The same type of thing happens with spiritual reality. Our understanding and willingness to live by spiritual law releases us from the perception that material law is governing anything real. If matter is an illusion, as Einstein said, then following material law would keep us operating in an illusion. Choosing to live by spiritual law reveals evidence governed by the laws of Reality and Mind, the true source of our very existence. The willingness to utilize our spiritual senses and look for evidence based on the operation of spiritual law brings us into alignment with the effect of spiritual law, the law of good, and we see more good — all possibility, all healing, all abundance, etc.

If we know abundance is a law of God, for example, it allows us to look for evidence of abundance when the physical senses tell us there's lack. Then our thought becomes open to ideas that express abundance, which leads to more abundance in our experience. An example might be making a purchase that aligns with feeling valuable or dressing differently because we feel differently about ourselves. We carry a spirit of abundance and worth and radiate to the world a different expression of who we are. People respond to us differently, see us differently, and we are considered for a job we wouldn't have been considered for otherwise.

Now see that in Spirit, everything is infinite. When we see that our identity is governed by divine law instead of the limitations of material law, this shift in our view of self changes what we see and changes our lives for the better. Remember Wayne Dyer's famous line, "When you change the way you look at things, the things you look at change." This shift in our thought of ourselves changes our lives for the better by allowing us to see more good — for more good to appear as real to us and for us to see what has been there all along.

Some would say, "But I can find lots of good following material law." Of course you can. In part because most people view the world and operate through a limited material lens. But the very premise of matter as the basis of reality is that it is finite and can't last. So good based in matter is not sustainable by nature and therefore can't last.

We want to understand how we interact with this divine law and how we practice it. This is science, Christian Science as defined by Mary Baker Eddy, the woman who discovered it in 1866: "The law of God, the law of good, interpreting and demonstrating the divine Principle and rule of universal harmony."

So much of what people know of Christian Science is about a religion, from pop culture references, or "those people who don't go to doctors." But not many know it as a science. And as you can see in the definition above, religion is not mentioned, though the whole Science is based on what we know of it from the Bible and Jesus' demonstration of it.

My own experience has been of something far beyond the physical healing aspects of this Science, beyond the Science as a particular religion. It has helped me better understand the way Jesus thought and operated, helped me to know this way of thinking is available to all of us through the understanding of spiritual law. He demonstrated it and embodied it completely. He knew his divinity, claimed it, and lived it. "I and my Father are one," he said. He called others to live in their divinity too, "And greater works than these shall ye do."

This Science is an approach to life, an understanding and perception of life as truly spiritual and based in God, Spirit. We get to be our divine self in spite of what the world claims about us or tries to confine us to. It's a way of thinking that's different from how the world trains us to think, or should I say, not to think. It opens the pathway to not blindly accepting whatever is in front of us and instead cultivating a disciplined way of thinking that looks deeper into the underlying spiritual reality of life.

This Science has very practical uses in our day-to-day lives. You can practice living under spiritual law, and utilize your spiritual sense, the spiritual interpretation of what you're facing, no matter what area of life you're looking at: relationships, employment, mental and physical health, finances, emotional well-being, social interactions, housing, intellect, education, everything! So no matter what the problem is, you always have the opportunity to find the solution using a spiritual mindset and demonstrate "the divine Principle and rule of universal harmony." Some of the most important advantages to this approach are:

- It's always available.

- It's free.

- It's proven and demonstrable.

- There are no bad side effects.

- The benefits from solving one problem generally have a cascade effect of solving other problems.

- We become better thinkers, kinder people, and more of who we were made to be in the first place.

- We become a better version of ourselves each time this approach is chosen.

EXERCISE

Let's look at the foundations of a spiritual mindset. Look over the elements below and note which ones feel natural to you. Also notice that this is not a comprehensive list. You may discover other elements of your spiritual mindset that resonate with you. Make a list of spiritual qualities that stretch you into fuller ways of being. Practice being aware of these qualities throughout the day and expressing them consistently as part of your mindset. Once a few are established, start becoming aware of additional qualities or ones that don't come quite as naturally. Add each and practice including it in your mindset until you feel comfortable with the discipline of all that you choose to include.

- **Understanding** — Understand that there is a power and intelligence larger than your own.

- **Willingness** — Be willing to recognize that the material sense is limited and that spiritual sense is unlimited. It sets us free. With spiritual understanding, we express infinite Mind — the all-knowing, divine intelligence — God's Mind as our mind.

- **Acceptance** — Accept that not only are we created with a built-in spiritual sense, but that we are also given the ability to use it.

- **Humility** — Recognize the true strength of humility that focuses on a higher power rather than little ego. Yield any willfulness, justification, self-righteousness, and condemnation or comparison with others. Have a grateful and giving heart that glorifies the allness of God, good.

- **Oneness** — Recognize that our oneness with the All is the reason that we exist. If we weren't at one with Source, we wouldn't exist. Thus the fact that we exist means we are at one with the divine. This means we can't get away from it or outside of it. We don't need to earn it. Our race, size, or intellectual capacity don't matter. Our social status, professional network, or financial net worth don't matter. We are at one with the Infinite. Period.

- **Belief** — Recognize that belief governs experience and is a firm and constant state. If we believe we are separate from the divine, our experience will follow our belief. If we believe our life is limited, we will see and experience limitations in every direction. And conversely, if we, using spiritual sense, believe and understand that we are unlimited, we will see and experience more freedom and possibility in proportion to our understanding.

When we accept the grace given to us by God and accept the fact that God does love us, we are saved from and freed from being or seeing ourselves as a condemned sinner. We are made free.

CHAPTER 9

Evidence of Spirit Over Evidence of Matter

Human consciousness equals human experience.
— Jack Hubbell

It took courage to ride my new buttercream Vespa, a 2003 "beater" with a brown leather seat and matching storage box on the back. Classic. When I bought it (such a great deal), it evoked romantic images of riding Vespas in Italy, tracing the curve of the Amalfi coast, white scarf trailing behind. But the reality was a bit different. The first time I rode it in the driveway, I ran it right into the side of my husband's car and fell over. It was like a scene out of a slapstick comedy, and we all had a good laugh. Clearly, more skill and practice was needed before I could pass the DMV's required motorcycle test.

After failing on the first attempt, I set out to build confidence based on competence. I practiced for hours doing circles and figure eights, drew chalk lines on the road in front of our house to test my accuracy and agility, and on the second attempt, passed the test easily.

By the time I'd been riding for a couple of years, I was used to commuting to work in Los Angeles traffic, up Beverly Glen and across Mulholland — both curvy and full of harried commuters and school car pools. I had no issue riding the right shoulder, passing cars safely and respectfully, falling into line whenever intuition guided.

I made rules for myself to feel confident and stay safe. Always wear your protective gear. Always listen to your intuition while riding. Always check your mental state before gearing up to ride. If I wasn't feeling mentally strong, I would drive the car. Do you ever have those days when you feel like hiding — going through the motions of the day and getting things done — but not wanting to be seen? Whenever I was having one of those days, I wouldn't ride.

Riding demands a mental stance of confidence in who we are and an ability to take up space. It may sound lofty to reference Vespa riding this way, but anyone on two wheels understands. If you want to disappear emotionally, you won't be seen by other cars, and that's dangerous! You might not think there's an instantaneous connection between the two states, but there is. The effect of our thoughts on our experience is direct. Riding when feeling vulnerable is dangerous. Riding when holding images of crashing is dangerous. Just as a negative mental state is translated into our experience, so the acknowledgement of our safety and ability is translated and seen in our experience. Riding while knowing our strength is safe. Riding while knowing our ability and intuitive guidance is safe. This particular day, I felt confident.

I got up on that clear July morning, and as I routinely did, stood in my closet wondering what to wear. I don't generally get intuitions about outfits, but I did that day.

"Put on white jeans."

"Seriously?" White jeans were not my go-to pants and would require a whole different level of confidence about how I looked in my body. But as usual, it felt like an intuitive prompt, so I followed it and wore them. Doing so demanded a level of internal confidence not based on external evidence or how I looked in white jeans. Paired with my chunky black riding boots and textured sweater, the outfit came together. I donned my black biker jacket that had been gifted to me a few weeks earlier by a woman I'd just met in the Vespa shop. Geared up with built-in pads and more protection than I'd had before, I rode my normal route to work.

When I got to the curvy part on Mulholland Drive, I heard a voice, "You're going down."

The thought alarmed me. It was the kind of thought that would come to someone lacking confidence, someone thinking or riding from the premise of fear. It was striking to me because I had done my self-check before I set out; I *was* feeling confident.

When the thought came, I had a choice. Take it in as a thought about me, or hold myself immune from the thought and not take it personally. I immediately rejected the idea of *going down* and claimed my safety and security as a divine idea.

I Looked Up to see the divine reality where there are no accidents, where the laws of good include all balance, strength, alignment, and harmony. Then I Looked In and affirmed my true nature and who I was as a reflection of all good qualities. I acknowledged who I was spiritually, steady and unchanging, unaltered by circumstance. I stayed with this line of thinking until I didn't fear a potential accident. Then it occurred to me to listen and be proactive.

"What if I needed to be alert to this and prepare? What would I do if I went down?" I asked myself.

I mentally reviewed all the motorcycle training. In my mind, I Looked Out and wondered what would it look like to be in alignment with safety instead of an accident? Stay relaxed, respond quickly and evenly, trust the brakes and use them firmly and gently, trust your gear and know you are protected, respond rather than react to the fall, roll and flow with the motion. Once I reviewed all the practical steps to take if needed (notice I was affirming what I would do and not saying what I wouldn't do), I let it go and reaffirmed my inherent safety. And I made it to work without incident.

I raced out of the office that afternoon. Someone had called interested in viewing our house, which was just about to go on the market. I didn't usually leave work at that hour so riding Valley Vista in daylight was a treat. It has lots of little rolling hills and bends in the road to lean into.

As I came to a favorite S-curve, up a hill and around a blind corner, directly in front of me was a massive white wall of SUV, spanning my side of the road, just sitting there! I was already leaning into the curve. I clenched the brakes, quickly, evenly. The bike went out from under me. I went down hard, helmet smashing against pavement. I continued gripping the handles, slid across the road, miraculously missing oncoming traffic, and skidded to a halt without hitting the SUV or anything else.

Time slows down in these moments. In the instant I realized I was going down, everything I had reviewed on my way to work flashed through my thinking — stay relaxed, move with the motion, trust your gear, but more than that, I was keenly aware of the truth I had claimed, and I felt a deep, abiding sense of being held in safety, that all was well, and who I was could not be touched or altered by this circumstance.

I chose to seek evidence of good and harmony

I immediately got up, righted my bike, which had impact and scrape damage on the side. Some parts were broken. I walked it over to the side to talk with the SUV driver and her car full of very smartly dressed women heading out to lunch. People rushed over with kind concern and advised me to go to a hospital to get checked out. I assured them that I felt fine. I went through a process in my thinking that allowed me to overcome what the senses were telling me by relying on what I knew to be true spiritually. Instead of checking if I was okay, I claimed I was okay.

Instead of looking for evidence of a problem, I actively looked for evidence of what I knew to be true based on Truth, what I knew based on Looking Up. Instead of looking at my physical body, I Looked In and affirmed that I was aligned and at one with the divine and that my true identity remained untouched by circumstance. My being-ness was intact, so Looking Out, only my true self could be expressed. Since I was at one with and expressed qualities of safety, alignment, balance, health, and wholeness, I couldn't Look Out and see evidence of a person separated from these qualities.

The driver and I exchanged contact information, witnesses came forward to offer video of the event, and the scene got resolved quickly after I declined an ambulance and police intervention. I made a conscious choice to get back on my Vespa and ride home to meet the potential buyer of our property. Settling on my bike, I noticed a hesitation surface, questioning if I was okay and whether the pain would kick in when the adrenaline wore off. I actively chose to rely on and take a mental stance of clarity and confidence. I affirmed who I was and rejected any ideas that floated by suggesting that I was damaged or traumatized or now had to fear other accidents.

Since what we focus on expands and what we seek evidence for is what we see and experience, I chose to seek evidence of good and harmony and continually focus thought in that direction. I chose love over and over instead of fear, wholeness instead of brokenness, and security instead of danger. I saw myself held and supported by Love instead of vulnerable and pushed down by fear and accident.

The next day, stiffness and pain tempted me to remember slamming down and scraping the road with my body and then tell a story of separation from good. Then I had an aha moment.

"What if this incident had happened six months ago? Would you be considering it now? If there's only now, and the past and future aren't real, doesn't this moment only include what is present in thought? Can't I claim now who I am unique from yesterday's story? And if I didn't consent to the idea that 'I was in an accident' yesterday, why would I tell that story today?"

I looked at my white jeans and noticed that the pants showed zero evidence of my Vespa and me going down on the street. There was nothing that would indicate my right leg, trapped under the bike, had scraped across the pavement from one side of the street to the other until I came to a stop. NO EVIDENCE! There was not one mark, dirt spot, smudge. NOTHING! To say I was surprised would be an understatement. So why was I prompted to put on white jeans that morning? Why did I have the premonition of going down when I rode to work? Why was I on that curve just then, racing home uncharacteristically during daylight?

I love having an example to share that gives you evidence of divine law governing. Even a glimpse of this law allows us to see it in practice. Our educated sense of reality is based on laws of matter, but these experiences give us a window into the divine law of Spirit. Spiritually-based reality trumps anything we've been educated to believe as material reality. What we see in our experience is based on our sense of reality. What we see in our experience is the expression of consciousness, so that which is held as true in consciousness is what we see in our experience. What we focus on matters. We need to ask ourselves, are we expressions of the One consciousness, including all and only good, or are we a separate consciousness creating and observing what we believe?

This is why this choice matters. We choose to align with and accept the outward evidence or choose to believe the truth based on Spirit, and then see evidence of that belief. Look Up, Look In, Look Out. I Am, I Can, and I Do, but as a reflection or manifestation of the All, not as a separate system operating on its own.

One of the things to take away from this experience is to notice what you do when you receive an intuition about something. Do you trust it and follow the thought to the end? When the idea presented itself, "You're going down," I didn't just toss it off and sit in my egotistic view of life, I yielded to the message and acted on it in two different ways. I actively claimed what is always true about me spiritually when I Look Up. I knew that my true identity couldn't be touched by accident or separated from the divine source of me.

Then I also got practical and applied the truth to my experience. It went something like this: If I can't ever be separated from the truth of who I am in Spirit, would going from vertical on a Vespa to horizontal on a Vespa change who I am? No. Would my at-one-ment or alignment with wholeness, strength, safety, and health change by going down on the pavement? No. Would my expression of dominion diminish because of a change of location? No.

Thought governed by peace and safety differs wildly from thought governed by fear and pain. A thought at peace is open to ideas that lead to what's safe and the expression of safety. Human consciousness equals human experience, but we also need to recognize that human consciousness can be lifted up to reflect more of the divine when we yield to the reality of the divine. This is where our choice enters the equation. Are we willing to yield to the divine reality, or are we determined to believe only what the material senses tell us and experience the limitation of that? The good news is the divine reality is always available to everyone, and we have only to turn thought to the divine to see more of the divine reflection as our experience here and now.

Safety is expressed in ideas that keep us safe, like having the idea to relax when needed, move a certain way to avoid conflict, or respond quickly. A fear-based reaction blocks out ideas of peace and safety. By clinging to ideas of danger, we tense up when we see an obstacle, let anger take over, and become aggressive, focus on the physical, and are limited by what the senses tell us is real. To return to the metaphor of the train tracks, how would we react if we believed they were actually merging together in front of us? Our fear of that "fact" would initiate a reaction based on the evidence.

Both avenues of thought were open to me, safety and danger. I chose safety, and until I found and felt a sense of peace with it, I reasoned that my safety could not be interrupted by accident. I stayed with it until the thought of "going down" didn't bring up any fear.

This is the necessity. We must be diligent in our thinking to not gloss over even the smallest temptation to see a problem as ours personally. When the thought of going down came to me, I needed to see that the thought was not mine and not for me. I had to choose to know this was not true about me; it was a suggestion that I could accept or reject. Seeing the problem or suggestion or temptation as impersonal is what keeps us from believing it as true about us individually and therefore keeps us unentangled from the experience.

Next time you feel such a problem or temptation rising, when the thought comes:

- Observe it.

- Recognize it's not personal. It's not yours. It's just a thought.

- Identify the negative suggestion as noise, chatter, or as a prompt to move you towards what's true.

- Listen for a true idea, an inspired idea, or intuition. Hear the message and mentally respond.

- Focus thought on what you want and turn thought away from what you don't want. This is very important because what you focus on expands in your experience. When we keep our thought focused on the truth, the truth cancels the lie. The power of truth is in effect. This is not a personal power. It is an individual choice to let consciousness reflect truth instead of negative suggestion.

CHAPTER 10

Love Casts Out Fear and Dissolves Hate

There is no fear in love;
but perfect love casteth out fear.
— I John 4:18

I was a night manager at an LA restaurant for a while in the late '70s. We closed at 2:00 a.m., and occasionally I gave Jose, the cook, a ride as it was easy to drop him on my way home. As we drove, invariably the conversation turned toward spiritual subjects and God. One time, there was an overwhelming presence of Love in the car. We were so moved and inspired by the conversation and palpable feeling of the presence of Love, we both teared up.

An urgent thought sparked in me, "Pull over!" I acted quickly on the thought and pulled over under an overpass on the surface streets of LA.

As soon as I put my green 1967 Le Mans into park, a homeless man emerged from the shadows and ran up to the passenger window. "I'm going to kill you!" he screamed, waving his arms wildly.

I saw the flash of something metal. I turned to Jose and said, "Roll down the window." He didn't hesitate.

I think back on this now and can't really imagine my response, but at the time, it was the only thing to do. There was such an overwhelming sense of Love in the car that both Jose and I felt completely calm. There was a power larger than both of us governing the moment.

The homeless guy lunged into the car, threatening and yelling. We felt no fear. I talked with him calmly. I don't remember the exact conversation, but I do recall mentioning that we'd just been talking about God and the power of Love. He said he was the devil and he was going to kill us. It was as though his words had no power at all, and I continued to pour love out to meet the verbal and physical assaults. I told him that God was Love and that he could feel this if he chose to.

Love truly does cast out fear.

Over the next several minutes, his demeanor shifted from anger and aggression to calm and curious. We expressed Love. It was the only thing we could express, the only thing present. The change was like the effect that light has on darkness. When light is present, the dark can't exist. Love truly does cast out fear. I remember his parting words because they seemed so unusual coming from the man who ten minutes before had acted violent, incoherent, and out of his mind.

He said, "I want to find out more about this God you speak of." Even the syntax seemed odd. That's why I remember it. And he walked away calmly back into the shadows.

What if I hadn't pulled over right when the intuition came to me? What if I'd waited? What if I'd driven away when he attacked the car and threatened us? I have no idea if our conversation had any lasting effect on the man's life. But what if it did? What if that was a turning point for him? We saw him change completely in a matter of ten minutes. What if that change was permanent for him? One can only imagine. But even the possibility that it had a lasting impression gives us greater incentive to follow our intuition anytime it comes to us. We never know whose life will be changed. I know that incident changed me, and based on our conversation afterwards, it likely did for Jose as well.

We both Looked Up, saw God clearly, Looked In and felt our individual oneness with the power of Love, immune to fear and hate, and Looked Out to see our experience morph into alignment with what we knew. The power of Love is palpable, impactful, and effective. Being able to Look Up in the middle of a tense moment and get out of yourself definitely takes practice. The good news is, this ability is available to everyone.

EXERCISE

Take a moment to recall a time in your life when you responded to fear or hatred with love. It's good to recognize the power of just one choice. When we look at our own experience and note these moments of shift, it empowers us to recognize the moment and make the choice again. If you can't recall a moment when you've done this, perhaps think of a time when you met fear with fear or hatred with hatred, and ask yourself if you could have responded with love. Would you have seen a different outcome? What will you do differently the next time you face fear or hatred? Will you remember you have a powerful tool and use it?

CHAPTER 11

Death Challenges — Eternal Life Wins

Life is eternal. We should find this out,
and begin the demonstration thereof.
— Mary Baker Eddy

When the space shuttle, *Challenger*, exploded in 1986, my world changed. I was living in Boston, producing a daily radio show called *Conversations with the Christian Science Monitor*. I honestly don't remember what the show topic was that day, but it didn't have anything to do with NASA or the *Challenger* launch with teacher Christa McAuliffe aboard. After the explosion, we pivoted fast. School children all over had just witnessed seven astronauts die right before their eyes. Shamefully, the media played the explosion over and over and over again. To support parents in dealing with their children's experience, we pulled together three experts: a child psychologist, a healing practitioner, and a child trauma specialist. The show came together beautifully. I was proud that it served a great need.

Still, I was completely unsettled, as most of us were. I had grown up to understand that Life is eternal, and I had just watched seven people blow up. How could I reconcile the concept that Life is eternal in the face of such catastrophe? Although I certainly knew that people only live on this planet for a period of time, this abrupt truncation of life was so startling and visceral, it shook my core beliefs about life as Spirit. The picture didn't match what I'd always known. I couldn't shake it and needed an answer. Was life eternal or not? How could life be eternal when this looked so final? I was angry and confused.

I reached out with all my heart and asked God. I needed proof that eternal life was real. Going to sleep that night, I felt like Jacob wrestling with the angel, and I was losing the fight.

Then I had a vision. I call it a vision rather than a dream when I'm given information rather than recycling my own thoughts. You'll understand why in a minute. I was an astronaut, dressed in the full launch suit walking across the bridge to the space shuttle, boots making the distinct familiar sound of our last steps on a solid platform. All buckled into our seats with helmets on, we waited. The countdown began. Engines fired, growled, and violently rumbled beneath us; the power felt awesome, almost overwhelming. We went through our protocols and focused on the tasks at hand.

Words can't describe the mix of feelings. Calm exhilaration, expectation mixed with confidence in our training, complete familiarity and utter newness at once, opposites playing on one another pulling my mind and body to extremes and landing somewhere in the present moment of dials, lights, indicators, readings, launch signals, and somewhere deep down inside, a quiet knowing that this was right, just as it was supposed to be. I was in my right place. Three, two, one . . . Lift Off!

And then there was a noise, an unmistakable high-pitched, squealing, gas-escaping-under-pressure noise. All I wanted to do was block out the piercing sound, but we couldn't get to our ears under our helmets. The noise overtook me and intensified. Then came the explosion, and all I can say is nothing changed! I was exactly the same. Same body, same mind, same feelings, same me. It was like I'd walked across a line on the floor. The only thing that changed was that the noise stopped!

Then in this vision there was a jump cut, like in a movie. I was standing on the beach across from the launch pad where all the families and A-list observers gathered to witness the launch from a distance. They were out of their minds, sobbing and screaming, or aghast in silence, stunned and in shock.

I stood right next to them, assuring them, "I'm okay. Everything's fine. I'm okay!"

They couldn't see me or hear me. I kept telling them I was fine and that everything was okay. I so desperately wanted to assuage their pain, lift the darkness, but the message didn't cross the divide between us — the gulf in consciousness. I yearned to send my feelings of lightness and joy to them, for them to truly know everything was okay.

That's really all I can remember of it. But the reason it changed my life was what came out the next day. The day after the explosion and the night of my vision, the media revealed what had caused the disaster. There was a gap in an O-ring that allowed highly pressurized gas to escape, which caused the explosion. The high-pitched sound of gas escaping under pressure in the vision the night before was a detail that told me (before it had been revealed), the cause of the accident and confirmed for me that what I had experienced wasn't just a dream.

Life is eternal. There is no death

I asked for an answer. I got it. Life is eternal. There is no death. Who we are doesn't change by what looks like death to the material senses. We are whole and eternal ideas in Mind, untouched by circumstance and accident. I lived through this experience that looked like a dramatic end of life and yet came out untouched, unchanged.

When I Looked Out and saw death, I Looked In but only felt confusion, anger, and fear. That didn't help resolve it for me. My only recourse was to Look Up. I asked God for an answer. I knew God was Life and asked to *see* Life instead of death. The vision allowed me to live through the experience to see that Life never stopped being expressed. Only the false sense of Life painted a picture of death.

Again, when it looks like there's a problem as we Look Out, we go back up the chain to find the truth. Look In to shift our view or perspective away from limitation and finiteness. If we still feel wobbly doing that, Look Up to see the limitless and infinite source of all, and see that allness reflected as us. This shifts our view, and in turn, our inner understanding and outward experience. The truth known and accepted countermands limited perception, and we see the truth reflected in our experience, negating what once looked like a problem.

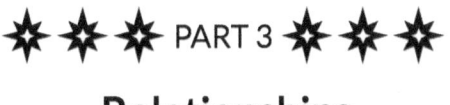

Relationships

Love is of God.
— I John 4:7

My deep desire to know God surfaced very early. I vividly remember standing in the bluestone entry of my childhood home, looking *up* at the brass front doorknob, trying to wrap my three-year-old little brain around a concept I had just learned in Sunday school that morning, that God is All and God is everywhere.

"Mommy, if God is everywhere, is He in that doorknob?"

I don't remember my mom's answer, but I do remember yearning to understand. That desire to understand God, feel God's presence, and hear God's voice has been life-long.

I remember being alone in the living room when I was about six, sitting in the blue chair in front of our black and white TV with a bunny-ear antenna and wondering, *If God is everywhere, is God right here in the room with me?* As soon as I thought of that question, I felt a hand holding my little hand and squeezing it gently. I felt a loving presence. I can still feel it today when I recall that moment. Love reassured me. I felt safe, certain of goodness, when I felt God hold my hand. I remember making a deal that I would always listen to what He told me and pay attention to that feeling of closeness and assurance of good.

The source of love is not other people; it's God, divine Love. People come and go. Love is constant and steady. When we look to people, circumstances, or material things to fill us up on the inside, we find ourselves in a constant game of chase and loss. When we recognize that there is one divine source, Love, it is always available to us no matter who is around or what our circumstances. Then when the outward scene changes, we don't feel like the rug just got ripped out from under us. We know our source and remain loved.

Is this easy? No! But the concept is simple, and we get better at feeling filled up from within by Looking Up the more we practice it. When we know all we need is at hand (Look In), we are free to express it outwardly (Look Out), and bless those around us. Let the love we express be the rich overflow of the love we feel inside, which is the manifestation of divine Love.

Relationships are a great place to see the effect of the frame we choose. We can align with love by following Up-In-Out or, if things seem off-kilter, we can recenter love in our life by going backwards up the chain to make the correction: Out, In, Up. If it looks like a problem is out there, the correction is not to reach out and fix it, but to Look In to correct and recenter. Adjust our own thought and what we claim as true. Clearly identify our true self and correct our view of others based on spiritual sense. If that is still wonky, Look Up. Get recentered on God as the source of all good and start from the top. Know who God is, then Look In and know who you are, and Look Out again with true eyes and know who others truly are. You will see what looks like a problem diminish in proportion to your thought being aligned with the divine, instead of the personal sense of power the little ego is trying to wield.

When people fall out of your life, you learn very quickly to rely on a higher power to feel loved. When we try to force people to love us, we experience the pain of that until we learn to let go of a personal source of love. When relationships are the expression of the one true relationship we have with the divine, there's more love, more freedom, and more abundance. We have a greater sense of goodwill and generosity, of seeing and being seen for who we really are. It feels like a miracle because it is. A natural expression of the divine reality.

CHAPTER 12

Rely on a Divine Source for Love

Patient woe; the human yielding to the divine;
love meeting no response, but still remaining love.
— Mary Baker Eddy

The summer before fourth grade was tough. My parents divorced, my dad left before my ninth birthday, and my sister and I got into trouble. The older neighborhood boys wanted to break into the elementary school. I tagged along, always wanting to fit in, even more that summer since Daddy had just left. We walked the path through the woods to get to Deer Hill School. But once we got there, we came to a standstill. The other kids gaped up at the building, wondering how to get in.

Wanting to prove myself a valuable member of this band of kids, I said, "I know how! If we can get onto the roof, I can get us in."

Since I was the smallest, they elected me to climb the eighteen-foot drain pipe onto the roof. Not considering the danger or the crime they were prompting me to commit, I scaled the wall to the roof, opened a roof hatch, climbed down the ladder into the room where I took trumpet lessons, and opened the front door of the school to let them all in. We went to town tossing papers around and scrawling on the chalkboards. We didn't cause any damage, but we did make a royal mess.

My brother, wanting to get back at me for exposing his involvement in setting the water tower on fire earlier that summer, told my mom, who informed the police. We had a nice chat with officers in the small town police station and much to my mom's relief, we were released with a stern warning and the task of cleaning up the sizable mess we'd created. News of this incident in our small town may have caused what came next.

Back in school that fall, I noticed two things. A heavy metal chain now secured the roof hatch, and my best friend, let's call her Brenda, completely cut me off. She had no contact with me, and I thought she turned everyone against me. I was ostracized, bullied daily, encircled, pointed at, and put down at recess. I walked home ashamed and crying every day.

"She's not being a very good friend and shouldn't treat you that way," my mom said, defending me.

"I know she's still my friend. I just know it, no matter how she's treating me," I defended her. "I know she still sees me as a friend," I said in part to reassure myself.

I'm not sure if it was early codependence or early Christly vision that carried me to this conviction. I refused to see anything bad about my friend. I defended her goodness inside my head and heart and in conversation with my mom or anyone else who said she was bad-mouthing me behind my back. I refused to believe it. I mean, of course I believed the words people told me, but I didn't believe in my heart she actually thought and felt that way. I would not let go of seeing her the way God saw her — as innocent and loving.

I mentioned the situation to my Sunday school teacher, and she shared a quote with me that I held onto throughout that year — a quote I lived with every day, one that gave me the strength to continue in my conviction. It's part of a definition of Gethsemane by Mary Baker Eddy, "love meeting no response, but still remaining love." And the other quote that I lived with was from a hymn we sang in Sunday school, talking about God as "My best, my ever Friend" (a poem by John Ryland). Having my dad and my best friend disappear from my life in a matter of months forced me to lean on what I had available, Love. I didn't see any other options.

I endured the cruel cold shoulders of my peers for all of fourth grade. Then one humid day in May, my friend who had shunned me and hadn't made eye contact with me all year, caught my eye across the cafeteria. She looked at me and nodded — gave me a head tilt towards the hallway — the universal signal to meet in the girls' room. My heart felt confirmed. I knew she was being herself — the friend I had held onto in my heart that whole year and refused to give up on — had just looked at me and nodded.

I pushed open the door, and she looked up at me, sobbing. "I'm so sorry for bullying you and turning everyone against you," she said tearfully. "Can we be friends again?"

"We were always friends," I said. There was never a question of forgiving her. I'd never seen that behavior as her in the first place; I had stubbornly held fast to what I knew was true about her, which was not the human picture presented. It was my masterclass in seeing a person rightly. When the false picture broke, it was like she'd woken up from a dream or a coma, and we could talk again as though nothing negative had transpired between us.

The reason I share this story with you is to show that sometimes leaning on God came out of adversity and having no other choice. I don't think I would have learned this lesson by choice. I learned it out of necessity. There are probably many of you who have faced adversity and found ways to cope, and those coping mechanisms became your way of being in the world. It just so happens that I learned very young for better or worse that God was the only parent or best friend that would always be there and never leave.

It takes courage to hold onto the inner conviction given to us from God when the evidence all around us doesn't support it. This is the perspective you get from choosing to Look Up. It takes perseverance and letting go of human will to lean on a higher power when what you crave is a human friend or parent. This is the perspective you get from choosing to Look In. It takes faith to know that divine Love is constant, ever-present, never faltering, always with us, and always loving and abundant. You reinvigorate your faith when you choose to Look Up. It takes humility to Look In — to forgive yourself, release others from your expectations and limitations — and then Look Out, seeing others as whole and good, as individuals who express love.

Love liberates us. Love is the power and gives us the strength to take a stand for ourselves and others, even when we don't think we're strong enough — love carries within it wisdom and strength to carry it out.

CHAPTER 13

Relationship Based on Looking Out

All that glitters is not gold.
— Shakespeare

Trials are proofs of God's care.
— Mary Baker Eddy

W hen one relationship ends, we yearn for something better. When this happened for me, I Looked Up to a higher perspective for guidance. I figured if Looking Up worked for finding an apartment, it would work for finding a partner. I made a list of all the qualities I wanted in a man — a long, very specific, list — multiple columns on several pages of a yellow legal pad. And because we attract what we express, I knew I needed to start expressing the qualities I wanted to attract. That felt easy. I knew my strengths and weaknesses and thought I knew where I needed to dig deeper.

Though I didn't see it at the time, the strategy I adopted was backwards; I looked out before I looked in. I wanted the relationship to look a certain way. I envisioned it and held it as my goal. What I wasn't doing was Looking Up and listening for guidance and Looking In to see if it aligned with me.

Within a few weeks, the inevitable effect showed up in my experience. I was approached by Jack (not his real name), a guy who said he'd been watching me for a while and wanted to ask me out. We attended the same church and worked in the same complex. He seemed perfect and had all the qualities on my list. (I didn't realize at the time that I was missing several critical qualities necessary for a healthy relationship.) We started dating. It was fast and fun. We shared water sports, spirituality, music, friends, intellectual banter, you name it. Everything looked perfect. What I didn't realize was that I was so focused on what I wanted the relationship to look like on the outside, I lost track of checking in with myself to be sure it was tracking on the inside. I Looked Out and didn't Look In.

We looked the part of a happy couple. I wanted strength, intelligence, and spirituality, and got strength, intelligence, and spirituality. But I didn't Look In to know what kind of strength, intelligence, and spirituality would complement my qualities, and I didn't consider the extreme possibilities of these qualities.

Inside this perfect looking relationship, how did I feel? I didn't Look In and check whether it aligned with my heart. My head, yes, it checked all the boxes, but I kept overriding the intuition that said something was missing, that there wasn't room in the relationship for all of me to show up. Here's how it played out.

No matter how good something looks on the outside,
if it doesn't feel right on the inside, pause

Signs of disconnect showed up very gradually. His need for control grew in little ways, where we'd go for dinner, his place or mine, what activity we'd engage in, which friends we'd hang out with, or what movie we'd see. It all seemed innocuous, but more and more I found myself yielding to his desires and not voicing my own. When I would have an opinion, his comments were negative or dismissive and chipped away at my confidence, and more insidious, I became unclear about what I wanted independent of his opinion. The little critical comments grew more and more frequent. I was tired of the slights and diminishment of my intelligence, but rather than argue, I'd let it go to have a good time and avoid a disagreement.

He was so good at winning any discussion, it wore me down, and speaking up wasn't worth it after a while. With his emotional and psychological diminishment of me growing, so did his temper and verbal jabs when I'd offer an alternate point of view or suggest a different activity for our time together.

Little by little, one small compromise after another, over the course of eighteen months, I gave away my sense of self, my desire to be fully me, my confidence, my ability to make a clear decision based on my intuition, and my ability to say no. By the time the verbal and emotional abuse escalated, the damage had already been done. I'd already lost myself. I'd always been an independent thinker and one who acted boldly, and I was still that person at work, but somehow when I was around him, I lost myself, deferred to him, and over and over, yielded to his incessant need to be right and win. After months of battles — little ones, ones you wouldn't write home about — I was tired of arguing and needing to defend every decision, choice, and desire, and I just gave it up, let him have it. It was exhausting.

By giving up all those little battles, I, over time, stopped checking in with my own heart to know what was right for me and gave away my right to fulfill my own desires. By doing that, I had given him what he wanted, complete control. When I found the strength to oppose him, he was so surprised by it, his reactions grew bigger to put me down faster.

All the while, we looked like the perfect couple on the outside. Everyone seemed to enjoy seeing us together and spending time with us as a couple. The darkness was reserved for our private times. He was the life of the party and always "on." Though my outward appearance didn't seem to change much to others, two chasms quietly grew. One was the divide between who I truly was — strong, confident, independent — and who I became around him: weak, insecure, completely dependent. The other was the split between the public me — full of confidence and capability with everything going right — and the private me: a wounded, flinching, gun-shy victim.

The only time I seemed to get a compassionate response from him was when I needed him and he was in a position of power or control. So I found myself feigning illness or struggles just to see a compassionate side of him. I knew I was doing it, and felt like I was in control of myself and him until one time when I feigned passing out. In my various attempts to get his compassionate attention, I had gotten really good at appearing to be passed out by slowing down my breath so he couldn't even tell I was breathing. I was doing this to myself, and it was getting dangerous. At one point he called the paramedics. They couldn't gain access through the condo's metal front door; they had to call a ladder truck to reach the third-story window of the brownstone and break into my condo to "save" me.

I realized things had gone too far. Once they were inside my condo, they had a protocol to follow and were the ones in control. They started doing tests, taking blood pressure and temperature, checking my eye response, the works. They insisted on taking me to the hospital to get checked out. Seeing myself through their eyes woke me up. I quickly turned the situation around, convincing the paramedics I was okay and demonstrating my strength and clarity of mind. After my vitals came back normal, they allowed me to decline the trip to the hospital.

I needed to distance myself from Jack in order to snap out of this growing habit of self-destruction. But every time I'd get a little bit of distance between us and start to feel some semblance of myself re-emerging, he'd insert himself into my life again and all the old habits of dependence would come rushing back in. It was like trying to walk out of the ocean while the waves crash over you and pull you back in. Sleep-deprived from the constant late-night power struggles with him and barely hanging onto the image at work that everything was great, I felt myself cracking under the pressure. The holidays were coming which meant working extra-long hours before taking any time off.

One late night, after Jack schooled me on yet another thing I was doing wrong in his eyes, I curled up in a ball on my bed in the corner of my tiny bedroom, sobbing and inconsolable. I couldn't stop. Jack became more and more angry that I wouldn't stop crying.

"Stop it! Control yourself," he shouted. "All I've done is support you and be nice. I'm here, aren't I? What's wrong with you? Stop it! I refuse to believe you're this upset. Snap out of it."

He picked up a spiritual book, one we had studied together, and whipped it with such force at my head, it almost knocked me out. I let out a startled scream, and something in me broke. My resolve and self-preservation were gone. I couldn't respond. It was only later I realized the irony — he quite literally "threw the book at me," a book whose counsel would have condemned the violence of his actions.

The only solution was to get away. I made the decision to go to the Benevolent Association, a place where I could get some rest without any pressure from work, Jack, or other people.

I stayed there for three days. The first two I spent alone and talked with God nonstop. Having another human in the room felt like too much pressure. I listened to the same two cassettes of calming and inspiring music over and over, one of them recorded by a dear friend, which made me feel very loved. I reached out to God until I was able to feel grateful for my life and all the good in it. Then I was ready to go home, back to work, and my routine.

The violence grew. The words were harsher, the emotional treatment more manipulative, and the physical control more frequent. Anyone who's been in a codependent relationship will recognize the twisted formula. The extremes revealed themselves more and more. As I grew further from myself, Jack and I grew further apart. I struggled to find myself and pulled away for periods of time, only to get sucked back in. The pattern repeated for months.

I share this, partially as a cautionary tale so that any of you who find yourselves in this situation might recognize what's happening and get out from under the landslide sooner, but also so that you might feel empowered to trust the intuition that keeps whispering something's not right and trust it enough to act on it sooner than I did. No matter how good something looks on the outside, if it doesn't feel right on the inside, pause, Look Up, Look In, and then Look Out again and see if things need to shift. I didn't do that.

Unfortunately, it took an act of physical violence for me to wake up. I went to Jack's apartment to talk things out and challenge his treatment of me. He utterly refused to admit to any of the verbal or emotional abuse.

"Can we please talk about this?" I asked, his body filling the full frame of his doorway.

He stepped out of the apartment and shut the door behind him, leaving us in the hallway.

"We have nothing to talk about. Go home," he said tersely. "Clearly, you're emotional right now."

"I need you to hear me. I want you to know how your words make me feel." I was grasping for acknowledgement. I had an overwhelming desire for him to admit his manipulation and verbal abuse, his incessant need to be right all the time, which was paid for by making me wrong. I desperately wanted to have a voice — to know that my view was valid. I needed confirmation that what felt off to me actually was off. But because I'd been groomed to seek validation from him, I was stuck trying to get him to agree with what I saw and felt. He went on the offensive, deflecting attention off himself and onto me.

"You don't see yourself, do you? Why are you so emotional? You must be having a bad day. Stop groveling for attention." His tone grew more aggressive.

"Can we please just go inside and talk?" I asked repeatedly, trying to move our conversation inside where I would feel less exposed and where I would feel he'd made some concession to my wishes.

"Get away from my door. Leave."

He grabbed me by my shoulders and physically forced me away from the door. I struggled to get free and go inside.

"I'm not leaving until we talk this out." This challenged his control. Bad idea.

126

He dragged me down a flight of stairs and then pinned me on the floor in the corner of his building's entryway. He pressed his knee down on my neck with the whole weight of his body. I couldn't move, and my leg was flaring in pain, having been injured in the struggle. I scrambled to get free, croaking out pleas for him to let me go before he broke my neck. I was at his mercy. He always liked being in control. This was the ultimate. He had the power and *granted* me freedom. I gasped for air as he released my neck, and he screamed some identity-negating obscenities at me.

Trembling, I collected all my physical, emotional, and mental strength to leave. I heaved open the massive 1850s solid oak door, hobbled down three stairs to the curb, unable to put weight on my leg, and propped myself up on a nearby stone wall, stunned and in shock. He didn't follow me, but the deafening echoes of his taunts and disgust dismantled me, rattled my core essence, left me in silent despair, in pain, and totally alone.

A passerby's voice jolted me into awareness of my surroundings. "Are you okay?" a young woman asked. "Do you want me to call someone?"

Still in the fog of shock and disbelief, I nodded her away as best I could. The nighttime sounds of the city, a siren in the distance, and the indecipherable hum of voices reverberating down this South End row of brownstones all felt very distant and unrelated to me. I sat in stunned silence, collecting myself.

Conditioned to think he was always right by his mental and emotional grooming of my submission, I searched recent events, scanning for evidence of my guilt, convinced I must have done something wrong to cause this. Embarrassed and ashamed, I coiled inward, yearning to be invisible to anyone else who passed by, and sobbed a jagged emotional cry as quietly as I could, still catching my breath. With tiny little flashes of mental clarity, I shakingly coaxed myself back into present awareness enough to limp my way home a few blocks away.

The next day at work when I looked up and saw him striding down the hall, my knees gave out from under me, and in that instant, I knew I needed to physically remove myself from the possibility of running into him. I immediately put in a vacation request and made plans to visit a friend on the West Coast.

I had been trying to extricate myself from the addictive bond, but I didn't love myself enough or feel worthy enough to see that I was accepting manipulation, abuse, and violence as a relationship. The disconnection and misalignment with my true self wasn't painful enough to wake me up and get me to act. The incident outside his apartment changed that.

When nobody else was there to lean on,
I was forced to reach higher.

The chronic nature of the problem became acute enough for me to finally commit to action and save myself. I'd been praying about it but still holding onto my own sense of control. I hadn't yielded to intuition. I still had a dog in this fight. I had wanted to hear him say he was wrong and admit his problem with control, but until I was more invested in healing myself than in getting him to admit guilt, I was stuck. Finally, I lost any desire to control him learning a lesson. I needed to learn my lesson. I made an appointment with the most spiritually intuitive person I knew, a professional healer who also happened to live in the same town as my friend on the West Coast.

I borrowed a car and made it to the appointment in this spiritual practitioner's office. We chatted. I was a mess. My tears filled the room. I felt completely defeated and drained. I honestly don't remember the conversation, probably because I was still in shock. But I do remember what he did next.

At the top of the hour, he announced, "I have to leave for the day. You're welcome to stay as long as you want, but would you be so kind as to turn off the lights and close the door behind you when you go?"

Panic raged in my body. My life raft just floated beyond my reach, and I had absolutely no strength to swim to it on my own. He left me there to drown. Feeling spent and helpless, I didn't have anything left inside to cry out. The heavy office door slammed shut on my hope of being saved. I was left curled in a fetal position on his floor, alone, truly alone. How could he leave in my hour of need?

Survival kicked in. I woke up to the reality of the moment. He wasn't coming back. And then the strangest thing happened: the only thought that occurred to me was that I'd borrowed my friend's car and had promised to return it in time for us to get to a church testimony meeting that night. The unselfed thought, this word I'd given my friend, prompted me to action. I was better in those days keeping my word to others than I was at keeping my word to myself.

As I followed this prompting and got up from the floor, everything in my thinking shifted. I attribute this entirely to the power of prayer. The spiritual practitioner's job is to see a patient for who they truly are, not for the messed up version of them that shows up in their office. Though I'm not even sure if he stated what he saw of me out loud when we met, I know that's what he was affirming of me, and this view of me healed me. It's a bit like the practitioner does the Look Up, Look In, Look Out about their patient. They see what God sees; they see the truth of someone so clearly, it has to be realized. I'm sure he saw through and beyond the mess I appeared to be at the time and saw my true innocence, freedom, and completeness.

He did good work. After he left the office, I'm sure he affirmed in his thought the truth of who I was. That I was always being communicated to by God and that I could know myself as God knew me. One of the issues I was facing or false beliefs that needed to be broken was that I was under the control of Jack or anyone else. Recognizing this false belief meant I couldn't be under the practitioner's control either. I wouldn't be healed of addiction by transferring dependence from one person onto another person. I needed to be dependent only on God.

The practitioner did the best thing he could by walking out the door. When nobody else was there to lean on, I was forced to reach higher. My only recourse was to ask God for help. I had no choice but to give up trying to fix it, drop the ego, the self-pity, the feeling of abandonment, and Look Up to lean on God and Look In to see my true divine self as God sees me. Leaning on others was a distraction from the true source of healing. My whole being shifted from anger to gratitude.

As soon as the thought shifted, I was free.

I woke up. I can't describe it any other way. I woke up from the nightmare of the prior year. In that instant, I felt like myself, something I hadn't felt in a long time. All the trauma, all the mental scars of codependency and abuse were gone! You know when you try to remember details of a dream that is fading from thought? It was like a fast fade in a movie. Everything was gone, and I couldn't remember the feeling of codependence on Jack. I was truly released from having any thought of the time with him. I was free! I felt lighter, conscious, even happy to be alive! Consciously aware of my true self for the first time in over a year, I was no longer driven by some outside force. It felt foreign, a welcome release, and truly miraculous.

Here are the elements that I believe brought about this healing of what felt like hypnotism, the haze of addictive thinking, and acting as a victim.

I had a clear desire to lean on a higher power and reached out for help from a spiritual practitioner to feel that power, since I was not able to handle the situation.

I was literally on bended knee on his office floor asking for help.

I was willing to listen for guidance and follow it when I was left alone.

I was determined to be true to my word to my friend about returning the car on time regardless of how I was feeling.

The practitioner doing his job meant he was claiming for me what I wasn't able to claim for myself during the time leading up to this — that I was already whole.

Though I had struggled with everything inside of me for over a year, this healing felt instantaneous. The shift in thought was so dramatic — it was a holy instant.

This experience made it clear to me that all the suffering was attached to the thought or the belief that I was stuck. As soon as the thought shifted, I was free. That singular moment has been one to look back on many times to help me realize that I'm just one shift of thought away from a healing. In this case I had the impulse to be true to my word and return the car. I acted on that higher thought and broke through the lie I'd been holding onto about myself. A lie that crippled my spirit and made me feel weak and a victim. Acting on a good thought freed me.

When we are brought to our knees by our own inability to help ourselves and reach out to a power larger than us, we open the door for the divine to step in. We leave room for God to be God and stop acting from our ego or that place where we edge God out. We Look Up, see the love of God as present. We Look In and see our true self as God sees us, humbly accepting the truth of that. And then we Look Out and see the evidence of our true self acting in alignment with the truth of us.

CHAPTER 14

Relationship Based on Looking Up

Divine Love always has met and
always will meet every human need.
— Mary Baker Eddy

I got up off the floor of the practitioner's office and returned my friend's car in time to go to the Wednesday testimony meeting at the church in Brentwood, and as was our tradition, since I was the one struggling, I sat in the middle between my two friends. About halfway through the service, movement pulled my attention to the side of the room. A man coming in late sat down at the far end of our row.

First impression. *Wow! Handsome!* And immediately the retort: *Are you kidding me, Lisa? You were just crying in the practitioner's office and literally pulled yourself up off the floor, and you're already looking at another guy?! Absolutely NOT!*

I consciously acquiesced to the sanity of no, but the thought persisted. Moments later, another thought, *You have to meet him.*

I fended off the temptation to fall immediately into another *wanting* outside of myself. Being new to feeling like myself after such a long stretch of absence, I wanted to protect the part of me that yearned to get my own legs under me and feel strong standing as me, without being defined in terms of someone else. Again I thought, *No!*

A moment later, it hit me. This persistent thought was an angel thought. It was steady and calm. It was present and didn't come and go. It was a knowing rather than an urging or push. It was clear and defined and simple. The more I humanly reasoned why this was a bad idea, the more the thought became a clear imperative. Because I'd just experienced the grace of healing and felt so complete and free,

I yielded to my life habit — obedience. I knew I would follow this intuition and meet him, but I did so under protest while my instincts and my brain screamed, *No!*

After the service, I resignedly walked up the aisle to where he was standing. His back was turned towards me and he was talking to someone else. I reached out to tap him on the shoulder just as a friend grabbed my arm and spun me around to say hello. I missed his shoulder by a whisper. I chuckled to myself and looked up. I shrugged internally to the angel, *I tried.* I had been obedient, and it didn't happen. I was off the hook. He walked out the door, which I thought was an exit.

Later, out in the parking lot where my friends and I were standing around catching up, he walked out of the building, passed by us, and headed for his car. I was caught off guard. I thought I had seen him leave already. I wasn't off the hook after all. By the time I asked my friend, "Jess, what's his name again?" he'd walked clear across the parking lot. If I was going to be obedient to the angel thought, I needed to act fast.

"J.!" I yelled, projecting my voice with confidence rooted in my obedience to the intuition. That caught his attention. He paused at his car door, turned around, and watched me walk towards him. He looked a bit bemused.

Sensing he wasn't sure if we'd met before, I reassured him, "Hi, I'm Lisa. I just got a really clear sense that I needed to meet you." His warm and generous smile gave me license to dive in. "So who are you and what do you do?" I asked in a disarming sort of way.

He leaned into my humor without skipping a beat. He told me he was working on a documentary. My antenna went up. Back in Boston, I was transitioning from radio into television, and the thought occurred to me, *Oh, this is a work thing; that's why I was guided to meet him!* I immediately shifted into work mode and set up a coffee for the next day.

That turned into dinner by the ocean and a stroll along the boardwalk. Though we went Dutch, which was appropriate under the circumstances, it didn't seem to match our chemistry. And when he offered me his jacket as it got cooler, I sensed he was paying attention on a different level.

I couldn't imagine him not being in my head

He drove me back to my friend's tiny Santa Monica apartment. It was popping with energy, the living room jammed with basketball fans watching game five of the NBA playoffs — Lakers vs Pistons. I rooted for the Lakers only because the Pistons had squeezed out my home team, the Boston Celtics, in the Eastern Division Finals.

I got up to use the restroom during a time out and stepped carefully through the fan-jammed room. On my way back, I came up behind where he was sitting in a chair and had a thought: I needed to place my hand on his shoulder to maneuver back to my spot on the floor. I thought, *If I put my hand on his shoulder and he doesn't respond, that's fine. But if he does respond, he's interested,* and then I'd know that this was more than a work connection for both of us.

When I rested my hand on his shoulder, he immediately brought his hand up from his lap and put it over mine.

It was on!

After the game, J. and I took a very long walk around a very short neighborhood block with lots of sitting on stone walls and talking and maybe a little smooching. When we finally returned to the apartment, everyone else had left. My friend had made up the couch for me to sleep on before she headed to bed. J. and I kept talking. By the time he left, I couldn't imagine him not being in my head. He had a permanent place in my heart. It was as if he'd always been there. He felt like home. I knew he was my husband.

Snail mail and long, late-night phone calls formed the rhythm of our courtship. I made a promise to myself that I would never call him if I was feeling needy. I didn't want to fall back into any bad habits. So I would call a friend or go for a run or a walk, anything but act out of neediness, insecurity, or codependence.

A few months into our courtship, on a particularly rainy and dreary New England day, I felt a yearning and loneliness I hadn't since J. and I met. I clung to my self-imposed rule and decided to go to the only place that would feed my soul, the beach. Sandy Beach called to me — I played there as a child and rode my bike there each day during the summer before ninth grade.

I drove fifty minutes down from Boston to my hometown and the deserted parking lot that stretched the length of the quarter-mile beach. The rain stopped just before I stepped onto the sand. My whole being reached for heaven to feel loved and valued. I felt emotionally vulnerable, and recognized the old pattern that had trained me to look outside of myself to find my value and stability. I knew not to yield to that temptation. Not yielding meant pulling hard in the other direction, and like the force needed to hold a tight turn in a go-kart, I pulled my focus with all my strength and turned toward God instead of a person or thing. I Looked Up. As I walked on wet sand left by the rain and falling tide, I started the conversation from where I was emotionally.

"God, I just want to feel loved!" I knew the source of love was God (Look Up), but I wanted to feel it tangibly (Look In). I didn't want to intellectually know it, be asked to rationalize, or take the reasoned approach to prevent falling back into bad habits. I wanted to feel it. Feel filled up by love. With tears and heaving breath, it felt desperate and a little pathetic. But that's where I was, and for once, I didn't force myself to be somewhere else to avoid the feelings or distract myself from facing the difficult reality of my state. I trusted God, but I was definitely testing the practical demonstration of this power.

I had the beach to myself and was grateful no one else was around to witness my red, puffy nose and literal snot-fest from all the crying. Everything around me resonated deeply — breathing the ionized air after the rain, smelling the salt, hearing the gulls and the lapping waves, and my absolute favorite, the rhythmic hiss of receding waves pulling pebbles back to the sea. I watched the birds fly and dart in the wind. The grayness suited my mood, and I sank into the yearning.

Walking slowly, still crying, struggling to let go of control and yield to divine will, I let go of the future scenarios or outlined outcomes of the relationship and any desire to steer the relationship to suit my needs and vision. I gave it over to God. When tempted to grab the controls, I remembered the horrible outcome of those bad habits in the previous relationship and quickly opted to let go. What I wanted was transformed into a higher desire — what God wanted — not my will but Thine be done. I clearly didn't know what was best and felt more at peace yielding than controlling. I released it all and trusted.

That's when it happened. Out of nowhere, a dog walked up from behind me and put his sturdy head under my hand. He was just the right height for me to stroke his soft flat fur without effort as I walked. It was comforting. Tangibly comforting. I felt my heart soften and my soul open. He stayed right with me while my whole system calmed and I stopped crying. Just then, a seagull cried, another of my favorite sounds. I turned my gaze to watch two gulls swoop in the wind above the waves. When I turned back, the dog was gone!

I looked up the beach. No dog. I turned and looked down the beach. No dog. The beach is only a quarter-mile long with big outcroppings of ledge rock at either end. The parking lot runs the length of the long side, and then there's the ocean. Nowhere for the dog to go. There were no people there, no cars for him to hop into, nor could he have run fast enough to get to the end of the beach. My only conclusion, as I recounted this to a friend later, was that I had experienced an angel. I wouldn't have accepted support from a person, too embarrassed by the way I looked from crying, so an animal was the only option for me to feel tangible love.

There's that great line by Mary Baker Eddy, "Divine Love always has met and always will meet every human need." I experienced the realization of that on the beach, and I was very grateful to know that when I Looked Up and turned to a power beyond a person, my human need was met fully from that point on. It shifted the source of Love for me from any person, place, or thing, to a divine presence, always available. And even when love does get expressed as a person, place, or animal, its source is always beyond them in the divine and therefore always present, powerful, and independent of proximity or form.

There's a lot to be said for knowing the power that's beyond us, the infinite, ever-present, and all-powerful divine — God, Holy Spirit, Source, Christ. Our life gets easier and simpler when we choose to know and understand that higher power. When we lean on God, we continually build confidence in our ability to trust that God's power is operating. If we would master that one skill — understand and trust the all-power of God — many of the struggles we face would dissolve as quickly as they arise in our lives.

Relationships with others may seem to fall under the category of Looking Out, but that depends on our approach. For some, relationships are used to confirm our own ego, sense of worth, and affirm our value and purpose. But if Looking Up and Looking In aren't firmly in place, then Looking Out — to others to find love or fill ourselves up with love — will never last or be the full representation of Love as it's meant to be. It will fall short because it's based on a personal, and therefore inherently limited, sense of love.

This is true when it comes to serving others also. If we think the source of our expression of love or support comes from us personally, we will eventually feel depleted and oftentimes resentful of the very thing that we think is filling us up. If you've ever experienced "compassion fatigue" this is the reason. Looking out to complete and satisfy ourselves, whether in relationships or service occupations, is a dead end. It will inevitably lead to burn out. It has to because the source is coming from a limited supply. But when we feel at one with or connected to an infinite supply of love in a relationship, whether that be romantic or professional service, we are filled up in the process from the infinite, and what is given as we Look Out comes from the rich overflow and never dries up.

If someone looks to you as the source, be alert. Always turn your own thought to the truth that the source is not you but the divine reflected or manifested as you. Then you are not personally responsible to supply the need; the need is met by you being the reflection of the infinite divine source, Love. One scenario depletes you and eventually causes turmoil with others; the other fills you up while you fill up others.

After a few months of letters and phone calls, J. made his first trip to Boston since our meeting. We drove up to Maine and spent a few days together. The morning after our first night, something felt off. We were out of sync and our communication didn't flow. We both questioned whether this relationship was what we thought it was. We felt unsettled and agreed to take our individual quiet time to pray about whether we would continue with our trip or go our separate ways.

Afterwards, we walked. My normal approach in a situation like this, when I intuitively know something is off, is to come right out and ask, and demand honesty and strength. But something stopped me. I can remember the moment vividly. Up until then, my tendency with men had been an attitude of *prove yourself, show me what you've got*. It was demanding, probably a defense mechanism that had kept me safe and perhaps a lingering habit from the former abusive situation. What happened next felt foreign.

Instead of an arms-crossed attitude, I found myself mentally opening my arms, opening my heart to possibility and vulnerability. I paused and listened to the silence between us as we walked. I felt compassion and patience in the space that I would normally fill with expectations — that the guy would show up strong and commanding. This moment held my future. I knew it. I felt it. The import of what came next would either confirm the deep knowing that this was my husband, or deny it. This moment was the fork in the road towards multiple futures.

After a palpably long silence, I gently questioned, "What are you afraid of?" That was a turning point. The love behind the question felt new to me. I had shifted inside. The moment demanded humility, patience, love, understanding, compassion, grace. I waited. I wish I had a recording of what he said after that. All I can say is that his words confirmed all the intuitive knowing that this was right and good.

CHAPTER 15

Marriage Lost and Found

You must be willing to give up the life you planned,
in order to have the life that is waiting for you.
— Joseph Campbell

The courtship progressed and led to marriage. J. was a freelancer at that time and moved to Boston where I had a full-time job as a news producer and anchor. The first few years of marital bliss followed the familiar path. We laughed and loved and grew in our careers. J. rebuilt our condo and worked part-time as a producer in news. I continued as a news anchor and producer. We were deeply in love, thriving at work, and enjoying life in the city with friends. But three years into our marriage, we faced a big challenge. The *Monitor Channel,* where we both worked, shut down. All the employees got laid off on April 15 after one day's notice.

I had worked at the *Monitor* for ten years, so the abrupt layoff came as a shock and also felt like an opportunity to explore new possibilities. As much as I loved broadcasting, news and politics were not my passion. During those years, I quietly yearned for work that focused on spiritual content and felt closer to my heart's calling — my love of Truth and Spirit.

As always, the process to find work followed the same pattern. Look Up to and acknowledge the divine, Look In and align my sense of self to include all good qualities and talents as a reflection of the divine, and then Look Out to be of service to God and see opportunities to give and express all of my true self as guided by Love. I followed the intuitions and leadings that came daily. Call this person, ask about this, research this. I listened and followed.

It's important to be humble during these times, to be faithful to the angel taps on the shoulder, to not question with reasoning, but to trust the heart's desires and take baby steps. Sometimes one little step, in what my head said was the wrong direction, was followed by a connection or interaction that guided me to the next right step. The result of this process led me and J. to work in Maine.

We got hired for the summer season at the International Film and Television Workshops in Rockport. I was an actor in residence and J. was a producer. We worked with A-list directors, directors of photography, editors, and actors from all over the world. The opportunities to work with incredible talent were enriching and enlivening. Mel Gibson, Alan Arkin, Ralph Rosenbloom, Don McAlpine, Billy Williams, Laslo Kovaks, Milos Forman, and the list goes on. Our work was challenging and rewarding, everything we'd both dreamed it would be. But our housing, provided by the Workshops, was less than ideal, to put it mildly.

We lived in the attic of a tiny house and slept in a bed that slanted to one side. The shower was nonexistent, and the charming white claw-foot tub lost its charm once we realized the only way we could rinse off with the hand-held sprayer was to kneel in the tub and duck down, thanks to the tub's placement under the steep pitch of the roof. The smell of mice never got resolved by the owner, and the couple across the stairwell in the other half of the attic, though very nice, had a very different schedule and always seemed to be up and chatting when we needed to sleep. Our sleep deprivation led to more and more arguing, which led to conversations about our growing frustrations.

I felt something was missing and I wasn't getting it from J. I wanted him to be more of a cheerleader, more gregarious in social situations, more positive. He seemed quite depressed and couldn't pull himself out of it. I had never spent much time at the bottom of the pool. When I got discouraged, I bounced back quickly. But J. seemed to walk along the bottom for long periods of time. It was challenging for me to empathize and emotionally draining to be in constant support mode, meanwhile feeling bereft of support myself. Of course, there were fabulous times mixed in, but the overall atmosphere of our relationship grew increasingly depressed. It seemed our marriage was not working, and I couldn't bear the thought of that, since we loved each other so much.

Looking back, I can see so many things I did wrong. I tried to fix my discontent on the inside by changing the outside. I wanted J. to change. I wanted our living circumstances to change. I wanted stability to come from others' assurances, from our relationship, and definitive future job options.

I was in complete limbo, suspended in a lava lamp of choices.

But what I truly needed was to Look In to understand myself better, and to do that I needed to Look Up to know God more as my Creator. Though my daily spiritual practice never waned during this time, I was blind to the truth that my attempts to smooth the frictions in the relationship were based on changing what was outside of me, rather than what was going on inside of me. I was not taking full responsibility for the feelings of discontent. We were both doing that in our own ways — Looking Out to fix things that needed to be fixed by Looking In.

At the end of the summer, I got hired for two films back-to-back, one in the Midwest and one in Los Angeles, while J. continued at the Workshops. He and I decided to see how things went during our separation and postponed making any decisions about where we would move or whether the marriage would continue. It gave me time to see the blind spot that had driven me to Look Outside myself to feel fulfilled.

After the films concluded and still feeling tentative, we moved our lives and broken hearts to LA. What did I want in this marriage, my career, my life? It felt like everything was up for grabs. When Looking Out surfaced more questions, Looking In brought answers. I got still and listened. Release came when I shifted to a deeper desire — to be of service to God — to listen and follow. But I wasn't sure what that looked like.

We settled into our place in LA, and an old friend of ours contacted me about a ten-day retreat of noble silence he was attending. I felt prompted to ask for details. It involved lots of sitting and walking in silence; no talking or eye contact with anyone the whole time. It started in a few days at a retreat center in the desert near Joshua Tree. Maybe this retreat was the opportunity to hear the answers I needed. Going within to listen to the still small voice was the only way to find certainty and know if I could fully commit to the marriage.

It's hard to describe the level of terror I felt. Nothing felt stable. I didn't know if after the end of going within, I'd be single or married, live in LA or somewhere else, or pursue a career in the industry. I was in complete limbo, suspended in a lava lamp of choices.

It's amazing how anticipating an experience with fear blinds us to the infinite possibilities beyond the threshold.

Three days later, I stood on a patio overlooking the desert scrub pines and Joshua trees. As I entered the great hall of the retreat center, vulnerability and fear overwhelmed me. I paused and reminded myself that going deep within was a sure path to clarity. I sobbed more out of fear than sadness, unsure where this journey would lead. Would I be guided to give up my marriage? I questioned my own existence and purpose. Did I have ten days' worth of thoughts inside of me? Would I be guided to a future I'd never considered?

The ego's anticipation of letting go brings fear, and that fear blinds us to the very possibilities that would make it easier to let go. The only choices I could see led to loss. My body curled in, creating a protective shield around my heart. It's amazing how anticipating an experience with fear blinds us to the infinite possibilities beyond the threshold.

To remove myself from connecting or communicating with others was the only way I would break the bad habit of Looking Out to find wholeness. The solution was to Look In, and to get clear on who I was and Look Up to my source. The answer would come from God. Thankfully, I trusted that wholeheartedly.

Three days into silence, I was seeing light bursts and hearing a voice very loudly, "Stay with your husband." Still feeling a bit rebellious and not quite trusting if I was getting *the* answer, I played the confusion card, *Do you mean my husband, J., or my husband, God?* The answer was obvious and by the end of the retreat, I trusted that staying married to J. was my path forward.

During the retreat, I Looked Up and saw clearly who God is, and I Looked In to know my true and full identity as God saw me. And then I Looked Out. The expression of that complete sense of self looked like marriage, a deep commitment to J., and a desire to start over.

J. had never faltered. Because he gave me the space to search within, when I was ready to commit fully, he was there to accept it. He had his own journey while I was away, facing his own demons, searching his own heart and sense of self separate from me and solely based in the Divine. Honorable men with good hearts and strong moral fiber show themselves when challenges arise.

We had a new marriage. I'm grateful that the path to healing and rebuilding included forgiveness for our own failings and a completely renewed sense of union, grounded in our highest individual selves.

We rarely argued, and when we did, we resolved it from a place of connection rather than separation, from looking within ourselves rather than looking at the other as the cause of the problem. Our love grew and found new avenues of expression, and I finally understood something J. had always known and demonstrated — true commitment. I was all in.

Exercise: Take Inventory of Your Relationship

When working with clients, I often ask, "What is the source of the love you feel?" The answer to this question can reveal their understanding of love as being a limited sense of love based on a person or an infinite sense of love based on God. Here are some questions that will help guide your own inquiry.

Ask yourself some very simple questions to check whether your alignment is first Up or Out.

Alignment Out before Up

- Do you feel people are the source of love for you?
- Do you feel less loved and less loveable when a person who loves you leaves your sphere?

- Do you feel loved less when people are not showing you love in the way you think it should be shown to you?

- Do you blame others for feeling less loved?

Alignment Up before Out

- Do you feel there is a divine Source of love?
- Do you honestly feel that when people and animals love you, the Source of that love is constant and divine?

- Do you rely on the higher Source of love to fill you up when an individual who loves you leaves your sphere?

- Do you allow God to control what love will look like in your life and let go of outlining what love should look like in your life?

- Do you trust Love to meet your need for love?

 CHAPTER 16

Intuition and Friendship

*Let yourself be silently drawn by the strange pull of
what you really love. It will not lead you astray.*
— Rumi

The deep lasting friendships and relationships in my life have been born out of intuition, beyond human contriving or design. When we meet people of our tribe, we know it; we feel it. We remember a bond that's already there, a familiarity. As Richard Bach says, "Rarely do members of the same family grow up under the same roof." Each profound relationship has included a deep knowing of bond and purpose at the start, even when the interactions didn't reflect that right away.

Right after my husband and I had our first child, I felt quite lonely. My best friend took a job overseas, and I found myself missing our day-to-day connection. Those were the days of expensive international phone calls.

True to my reliance on the divine for support, I sought a solution in prayer. I affirmed that my desire for friendship was legitimate and followed the process: Look Up, Look In, and Look Out.

I recognized that the qualities I experienced with my friend were not sourced in her, but in God. I loved her expression and our connection, but knew I couldn't be without companionship and friendship just because a particular person wasn't local. I'd gone through the same practice years before when I yearned to have a boyfriend. I listed all the qualities I liked in a friendship and claimed the source of those qualities as God. I knew I, too, included and reflected those same qualities and would see them in my experience.

When we are clear about the spiritual nature of our desire, nothing material can inhibit it. Our experience must conform.

My husband and I received an unusual invitation to visit with a couple at a desert resort along with friends of theirs, two other couples we hadn't met. We had a one-year-old baby, and it sounded less than appealing to spend a summer weekend in the desert. My reasoning brain was screaming, *Not on your life!* Yet it felt right to go, and we committed to it.

All three couples and our little baby in a stroller gathered for dinner the first night. Since I was on baby duty and she woke up at the start of dinner, I didn't get to know the other couples. The next morning, we all met for a walk around the enormous property of rolling green hills. One of the guys was an actor of note, very animated and funny, full of stories. I found myself walking next to one of the women I had barely said hello to the night before. I knew her name. That was about it. We walked along listening to the others behind us telling stories and laughing with them. She and I both walked quickly, and our distance from the group grew. As we came over the rise of a hill, both looking straight ahead in silence, a question crossed my mind. It sounded so crazy. I argued with the thought. *That's nuts!* I told myself. *Don't ask that.* But the question wouldn't go away. It had to be an intuition, so I went with it.

"Don't you think if we really wanted to, we could step off this hill and fly right now?" I asked, staring straight ahead, walking in an unconscious rhythm with her.

"Uh huh," she said matter-of-factly, still looking ahead, as though it were the most natural question in the world. In that instant, I knew we'd be friends forever. The moment confirmed everything for me — our deep natural understanding of reality, our rhythm and connection that didn't need to be expressed in words, a speed of processing and humor that naturally flowed and matched, an ability to leap frog over physical appearance and smallness to acknowledge the power of the great unseen, and a willingness to go with the moment without explanation. This moment confirmed what I could take for granted,

150

what needed no explanation. These elements formed a foundation for communication between us with no need of cultivation or tending. It just was. Like the given in a math proof. The elemental truth upon which all the rest relied, and the beautiful beginning of a friendship. After our weekend at the resort, there was a distance with Mel at first, a dynamic of unavailability. Several years went by before our lives and availability matched our connection. I kept trusting it was inevitable and followed the intuitive hits that came along the way. We took an acting class together, we visited with mutual friends, we shared favorite restaurants and food, exchanged gifts on holidays and birthdays, and laughed and talked about relationships, metaphysics, and life — always fascinating, intelligent conversations infused with our favorite passages from books and stories from our pasts.

Intuition delivers the memo of a friendship's depth way before the practical steps are taken to create it. This happened with my two closest friends. I felt and knew the connection in an instant, and then it took years for the friendship to match the vision. I'm glad I haven't been bothered or put off by this. I trusted it and had patience. At times it felt like standing watch outside the door, tending the lamp of the bond until the door opened to a deeper trust.

What's been true from the very start of Mel's friendship was the utter lack of competition. There's so much generosity of spirit and support on both sides, we're constantly saying and demonstrating the concept of mirror-mirror (a phrase Mel taught me). We see in each other the absolute best and want the absolute best for one another. It is truly a model for a relationship that is loving, generous, unselfish, and wildly supportive.

One time, before we were in a day-to-day rhythm of friendship, I got a very clear message to go to her condo. I knew where she lived but didn't know exactly how to get into her secure development without my name at the gatehouse. It was dark out and pretty late to be making a house call. I felt a very strong urge to go to her condo and knock on her door. Sounds a little creepy, but the message was clear.

I drove into the darkness and found my way to the gated development. I missed the entry gate and by the time I noticed, I was passing an exit gate. Someone was driving out just as I approached it, and I drove in before the gate closed. I found a place to park that looked unreserved for residents and started walking around, hoping something would stand out. I'd only been to her place once before so nothing looked familiar, particularly in the dark. I didn't even know her unit number. I listened for any nudges to point me in the right direction. I trusted the feeling of being guided in the right direction. There was nobody around to ask.

As I passed one building a second time, realizing I was going in a circle, something clicked. It felt familiar. I trusted that feeling. Then I noticed a patio outside a unit with a tree. The configuration resonated. I stopped, walked up to the door with the light shining out from inside, and paused before knocking. Was I absolutely sure I wanted to do this? What if she didn't want to see me? What if she was busy or had someone over? What if this seemed stalker-y? She was a well-known series actress who I was sure had dealt with too-eager fans. What if the semi-distance that we'd experienced up until now was the way she wanted things?

I put all those completely legitimate and reasonable questions aside and listened deeply to what I was being prompted to do. I knocked. Nothing happened. No one came to the door. I knocked again. Nothing. All the questions came rushing back and the self-doubt started to set in. But when I listened to my gut, tuned in to that still small voice inside, I felt an undeniable certainty that I was supposed to be there doing exactly what I was doing. I knocked again and put my ear to her door. I heard muffled crying.

"Mel?" I called out. "I got an angel message that I was supposed to come and help you."

I heard through her wail to come in. The door was unlocked. There she was, lying on the carpet, an emotional wreck in a puddle of tears. She and her long-time boyfriend had just split, and the darkness and loss engulfed her. Looking up with tired eyes, she revealed simultaneously disbelief and relief at my presence along with a poignant vulnerability and desire for a steady hand to lead her out of darkness, a familiar mix of emotions for anyone who has dealt with loss.

She had lost her dog, Tessa, not long before this, and it was all too much. After listening, tending to her broken heart, plying her with warm tea, and finally moving her off the floor, I reminded her of something I shared when Tessa passed. The love Tessa expressed was sourced in God. Unique, but the source of that love was beyond the things of form in time and space, beyond Tessa. And the same was true now with her boyfriend. He expressed all that love, but the source of that love was beyond him and was therefore all around her and ready to appear in a different form. Love is always there, waiting to take shape in our life.

The need for love was filled by a squirrel.

She had experienced this firsthand with Tessa. Once she understood this concept, within a few days a squirrel showed up on her patio — and again the next day and again the day after that. She put out nuts for it, and each day it would come to her patio and visit, eventually eating out of her hand. Months later, the squirrel visited her with its babies. The need for love was filled by a squirrel. You never know how it will come about.

If we're open to the need being filled, we will be more apt to see it appear in a way that makes sense to us at that time. Just like when I was upset that time on the beach and reached out to Love and the dog appeared out of nowhere. The love of the dog perfectly met my need in the moment, just as the squirrel perfectly met Mel's need in that moment of Tessa's passing. And now in this hour of need, Love would find her in a way that was comforting and sustaining. After all, I had been guided to her place late at night when it made no sense. Love was meeting her where she was, and the form of comfort she needed appeared on her doorstep.

Are there times when we don't trust that Love is available to us or we're blind to it because it looks different from what we expected?

It takes practice to trust the power beyond the 3-D-5-S world (three dimensional, five senses). It takes listening to our intuition and following it when the stakes are small, and that way we won't get emotionally, physically, or socially hurt by a failed attempt. Each time it goes right, and our intuition is confirmed, we'll build confidence to follow it the next time. Then when we're in the middle of a conversation, and a thought comes to us to mention something or take an action, we'll go with it instead of questioning and skipping over it.

Many times I didn't voice or act on an intuition that came to me for fear of being wrong, looking stupid, or sounding crazy, but with enough practice, I found ways to share the out-of-left-field ideas that floated through, always in the same way. Let's break it down. Notice how the ideas show up, what they feel like, and how you feel when they do. As we mentioned in an earlier chapter, intuition has a specific tone to it that will be consistent but also unique to you. It won't necessarily show up the way it does for someone else. Get to know the way it presents itself for you. Begin to trust your own version and be on the lookout for it.

Friendships based in authentic connection open the door to sharing intuitive information with no hesitation. It happened one time while I was catching up with another girlfriend I hadn't seen since her divorce. We sat sideways on the cushy white couch, one arm draped over the back of it, facing each other. She laughed about dating three different guys with the same name. Strange coincidence but easy to answer the phone without worrying who it was. Mid-chuckle, I got a download of knowing. I felt something important was coming. I knew whatever came next needed to be spoken. It's in those moments that

I lean on experience and allow myself to be brave and speak whatever comes, whether it makes sense or not. Confidence based on practice is the only thing that separates those who experience this from those who don't. Some are not willing to listen for it, risk saying it, or act on it once they hear it.

"You're going to meet a guy in the next three weeks, within six months you'll be engaged, and within a year you'll be married," I said.

Am I out of my mind?! I thought. *This sounds way too extreme and specific.* The information kept coming.

"You're going to live west of here."

At that point, I started to see a movie play in my head; the point of view was from a car driving west on the 101, Ventura Freeway, and took the Westlake Boulevard exit.

"You'll live out in Westlake."

The movie took me off the Westlake exit, turned left over the freeway, and right on Potrero Road. At that point, I thought, *This is ridiculous. This is the way to my friend Mel's house,* and I almost stopped the movie, discounting it on that basis. But just before the familiar bend up the hill to Mel's, the movie made a right turn into a gated housing development.

"And you'll be living in a house in this development," I said, describing what I saw in my mind-movie.

She sat and listened to this description and smiled. We both giggled at the certainty of my delivery, accepting it more like mild entertainment than a real prediction — though we did both admit a whisper of desire to commit the details to memory just in case they actually came true.

She met a guy two weeks later, they started dating one week after that, got engaged at six months, and were married within a year. He lived in the gated housing development where the mind-movie had guided me, and she moved there after they were married.

This experience was a confirmation — it gave me more confidence to trust these types of thoughts when they came to me. I noticed the type of feeling and type of thought that carried such intuitive information.

See if this resonates with your experience of intuition: It is present tense, peaceful, singular, calm, certain, clear, and simple. And notice what it isn't. It has no judgment, emotion, opinion, doubt, attachment, fear, stress, or manipulation.

We all have this ability to know more than we consciously allow our awareness to take in. It's based on what we see when we Look In. We will experience this knowing in proportion to our acceptance of our true self, made in the likeness of the divine, all-knowing Mind, God. Since we are all reflections of the same Creator and all made of the same "one suchness" as Alan Watts talks about, doesn't it make sense that we would all have access to the same knowledge and understanding? Wouldn't that explain why inventions and ideas and discoveries often come to several people at the same time? We can think of it the way American poet Ruth Stone describes the poem sweeping across the field, and she must race home to write it down before the poem goes on to the next poet. Or, as Einstein said, "I want to know God's thoughts. The rest are details."

What if we all hone our capabilities to hear intuition and the knowing of All? What possibilities would open to us if we knew the ideas of Mind? Or more accurately stated, if we knew we were the ideas of Mind?

Service and Self-Worth

Why are we here? What's our purpose? What am I supposed to do? Who am I?

We all ask the same questions, and we each need to find our own answer. Experience teaches us if we listen.

As these stories have shown, I've felt most fulfilled and satisfied when I've allowed myself to be guided by the divine. When I've been of service to a higher ideal and walked the path of yielding, I have fulfilled my purpose — to be who God made me to be and serve God in my highest capacity. For me, fulfilling my purpose, serving God, and self-worth have walked hand-in-hand.

I wonder if you have experienced this in your life? I wonder if you can look back and see those moments when you've felt you were being your best self — who you were called to be — and if those moments led you to serve others at a higher level? Can you string those pearls together and see a pattern? Aren't those moments the reason we're here? To love and support each other to the best of our being and capacity? Sometimes the opportunities to serve others come to us as a fleeting intuition, an offering. And when we resist it, don't believe it, or are not brave enough for fear of looking ridiculous, we miss the opportunity to be guided, to serve, and be utilized by the divine hand.

When we are filled with the thoughts of the goodness of who we are and grateful for the good present in our life, the good grows, and we start to see more good all around us. This isn't just positive thinking. This is our thought as a reflection of our oneness with God. God is Mind. There's only one Mind, God, and because God loves us, our mind is governed by God. We can yield to God's control, divine intelligence expressed as our consciousness. So the question becomes, what can we do to keep our thoughts focused on the good we desire? Go back to the same approach — the Up-In-Out Way. Look Up, Look In, Look Out.

Look Up: Lean on a power higher than your personal sense of life, the power of Life, God. Life creates and sees all good. Life created you for a reason. Don't you think Life has a vested interest in you filling the role Life designed you to fill? Why not lean on that infinite power and let it show you the way? Acknowledge that there is a divine force governing all and get out of its way. Look In: Acknowledge who you are and that you are made from the same source of all that is good. Claim that who you are is a reflection of that goodness. Then, Look Out: take bold committed action from that standpoint of goodness and see others as coming from the same source of good. Assume that Love is all and Light is all, and there is no fear or darkness. See the good.

CHAPTER 17

Give What You Are Given

Freely ye have received, freely give.
— Matthew 10:8

I was late, racing to attend the grand opening ceremony of a media academy my husband had created. Forgot my camera. "Dang it!" This was before we had cell phones with cameras in them. (Many of you reading can't even imagine that!) I made a quick stop at a local drug store to get a disposable camera. While in line, I overheard a customer talking with the clerk about their mutual friend who had just been found dead after having been missing. I was prompted to reassure them of the inevitably of life and that we are guided to know what we need to know. I shared a recent experience.

A few months before, I'd received an urgent call that someone had gone missing on a lake and was presumed drowned. That night I had a vision about where they were. I described the location to the family. They recognized the location but said, based on the evidence, it wasn't possible that they were there. Thirty days later, they were found where I'd seen them in the vision.

A tall gentleman next to me turned very abruptly and leaned towards me with intensity, "So, you're psychic!"

I was taken aback by the force of his declaration, stumbled a bit with my words, "Well, I don't know. I just trust what I hear, I guess."

"What do you see about me?!" he fired back, his gaze fixed on me expectantly.

"It kind of shows up or it doesn't. I'm so sorry, I don't see anything for you."

He turned to take his change from the cashier and left the store disgruntled.

I completed my transaction quickly and left. Walking to my car, I looked up and saw the tall man walking toward his car on the far side of the parking lot. The instant I saw him, I got what felt like a download of information — stuff that didn't make a whole lot of sense to me but felt very powerful.

I raced across the parking lot to deliver the message to him. "Wait! I just got a message for you!" Without waiting for his reply, I launched into what was there — sometimes for me, it's a bit like seeing the details of a dream — I need to speak it before it dissolves. "You're facing a big decision in your life, and you've been afraid to make it."

He nodded in confirmation. He still looked a bit apprehensive and, at the same time, hopeful.

"You have two options. One choice feels easier, one feels scary and hard."

He started to well up with tears. I looked him in the eye, saw affirmation, and kept going.

"You need to choose the one that feels scary and hard. You have all you need to go forward and will see how it all fits together after you decide. You'll remember this conversation years from now." I listened for more of the message. Nothing. None of it made any sense to me. There were no details, yet he seemed to know exactly what I was talking about.

He nodded again, tears streaming down his face, "You have no idea what you've done. What you've given me. You've changed my life! This will change my life! Thank you! Thank you!"

I walked to my car without getting his name or details of the life-changing message. I carried on with my day, driving to my husband's opening ceremony, disposable camera in hand to capture the momentous occasion.

Again, think about how many opportunities there may be in your life. When can you more actively Look Up and be aware of that higher knowing, Look In to feel how it resonates with you and filters through you, and then Look Out to see the opportunities to share what you know? Become present to the opportunities. You, too, could change someone's life. You may be the message carrier someone's been waiting for. Don't sell yourself short.

You will find graceful ways to approach strangers without freaking them out. You will find ways of getting past the fear of embarrassment. You will become so focused on serving others that none of that will hinder you from being utilized for the higher good.

CHAPTER 18

Listen, Trust, and Follow

And it shall come to pass, that before they call,
I will answer; and while they are yet speaking, I will hear.
— Isaiah 65:24

I used to play tennis almost every day. One afternoon, hustling to get out on the courts, my then boyfriend and I ran down four flights of stairs to the street from his Boston Back Bay apartment. Just then, I got a very clear message — a strong feeling and thought — that I needed to go back upstairs and call my friend in California. She was the kind of friend I talked to several times a year but not day-to-day. When we did talk, it was as if no time had passed. I wasn't sure why she came to mind so strongly. When I mentioned it to my boyfriend, he was surprised and asked if it could wait until after tennis. But I felt compelled to call her right away. He patiently acquiesced, and we walked back up the four flights to his apartment and the landline phone. Once upstairs, I realized I didn't have her number with me. I paused and reached out in thought to see if I could remember. Then, the strangest thing happened. A number came to mind that wasn't at all familiar. Though I didn't know hers by heart, I recognized that this wasn't her number. I dialed anyway. When someone answered, I was actually a little shocked to hear a familiar voice on the other end. "Tara?" I said.

"Lisa?" Surprise filled her voice. "How did you know to call? How did you get this number?"

"I just got a really strong thought to call you, and the number just came to me. Where are you?"

"I'm at David's place. He's not here. I'm just sitting here on the edge of his bed, and honestly I don't see any reason to keep going."

She was obviously having a really hard time and definitely didn't sound like herself. I was glad I'd reached her. She talked for quite a while about her recent challenges and reasons for the darkness she felt. Being three thousand miles away, all I could do was listen and offer assurance that she wasn't alone, that Love was right there beside her. She seemed comforted and started to sound like herself. The direness of the situation had passed, she assured me she was okay, and we got off the phone. The tennis window had closed, but that afternoon, intuition guided me to a more important activity, calling my friend. The priority was clear. When an angel tapped me on the shoulder, I followed.

Establishing each day with a Look Up, Look In, Look Out approach prepares us to be moved and directed by a power larger than us personally. When we yearn to fulfill a higher calling and be of service, we will be utilized, and not only will others' needs be met, ours will be too.

CHAPTER 19

Get Past Self and Let Love Meet the Need

Love is impartial and universal in its adaptation
and bestowals. It is the open fount which cries, "Ho,
every one that thirsteth, come ye to the waters."
— Mary Baker Eddy

Many of us at one point or another will face the privilege and selfless work of supporting an ailing relative — a parent, a spouse, a child. How the individual decides to get treatment is up to them. It's up to us to support them in whatever way reduces fear and envelopes them in love. Even if the picture looks different from what they or we are accustomed to, love is still the power that heals. We can stand for that no matter what and know it has an effect.

When my mom had heart surgery, it was natural for her to stay with us during her recovery and recuperation. I loved my mummy and would have it no other way. The sleepless days and nights leading up to surgery, the days in ICU, and the months that followed brought out in me a new level of unselfed love that surpassed even what was needed when our children were newborns. I reached a point when I had nothing left. There was no way to manage without Looking Up to a power higher than myself. And somehow, when night turns to day yet again, we're given the grace to keep going and be there for our loved ones. Moments when we're asked to reach beyond our own will or needs for a higher calling get seared in memory.

Mom had been home from the hospital for about a week. We had settled into a routine, but I was spent. I came up from the back of the house and saw her sitting in the great room waiting for lunch. I was in the hall just about to enter the space. I paused, exhausted, leaned on the wall, and readied myself for the next wave of service. The moment demanded that I get beyond self, not think about how tired I was after so many weeks of no sleep, not think about work and all that was piling up that I'd have to face later, not feel the ache in my body from the physical lifting and moving, not heed the responsibility I felt for all that my husband sacrificed for me and my relationship with my mom. I pushed off the guilt and shame for not doing everything perfectly or figuring out a way to do more. The list could go on, but it stopped.

In a holy instant, I Looked Up and asked for guidance. The only way to walk in that room and do more was to lean on Love. My love for my mom was sourced in the infinite well of Love and could never run out. Looking In and claiming the source of Love beyond me personally gave me strength. I Looked Out to see the expression of that Love realized. I paused, took a breath, put a smile on my face, and entered the room, asking what I could do to support and serve. Looking Up to find the strength in that moment came from a place outside and above me. It came from Love itself.

There is nothing other than Love that got me through those months of serving at such a deep level. I was honored to have the opportunity and cherish the time we spent together, but I also recognize that most of the time I was out of my body and operating on a different level just to survive. When I Looked In, it was to see myself as the manifestation or reflection of the divine and not as a separate source of love or strength. I put myself aside to Look Out, and let the overflow of love serve others.

The round-the-clock care took everything I had. And there was no time I could get away. Then one morning, I had a thought, *It would be so nice to take Mummy outside in the sunshine. But I'd need a wheelchair for that.* I'd been wheeling her around in an office chair with arms. It was a great solution, especially in the small bathroom because it allowed me to swivel her in place without having to do a five-point turn with a wheelchair. But when I considered the idea of going outside, the wheelchair would be the only way.

166

I let it go and the day progressed with breakfast, clean up, shower, hair, dressing, lunch, clean up . . . and then there was a magical moment when J. was home at the same time Mummy was napping, and I had a glorious opportunity to go for a quick run, which I hadn't done in weeks. I was so excited to feel the sun on my face and get outside. I raced to get in my running clothes in record time.

Out the front door before the opportunity passed, I stood at the gate to the street and paused to listen. Feeling grateful while I stretched out, I Looked Up and tuned in to that higher place of wisdom to listen for any guidance for this run. I heard that I should run a different way than I normally would. I was to go right, turn right, and in half a block turn left. I followed the directions, checking in with my intuition as I approached the street that departed from my normal route. I Looked In and checked for a feeling of confirmation that I was going the right way. I felt certain.

I wonder why I'm supposed to run this way? I asked myself, while at the same time confirming I made the right choice. Half a block later, I had my answer. There on the side of the road were not one, not two, but three wheelchairs put out for the trash pick-up later that day. I had my choice of one with foot rests, one with arms and no foot rests, and one with both. I tuned in to intuition again to make the selection. The micro view of that is always Look Up, Look In, and Look Out. The answer was obvious in a moment. I wheeled the chair home and left for my quick run on the normal route by the LA river in the opposite direction.

The desire I'd had earlier that day was quiet and heartfelt, sincere and unselfed. My motive was to bless my mom with some time outdoors in nature and sunshine, which is healing on every level when you've been in ICU, hospital rooms, and then indoors at home for weeks struggling to find a basic rhythm of independence and self-care.

When we are in the habit of Looking Up, Looking In, and Looking Out as the pattern of thought for everything, the result of that practice is sometimes evident in surprising ways. Our experience aligns with balance and harmony. We find that supply meets need. We're led to good with exact timing and precise locations. When my thought was aligned with seeing and serving the greater governing force of one Mind, also known as Love and Truth, or God, my experience was better and expressed more Godlike qualities. What is held in our consciousness is seen in our experience. Anyone can practice this.

CHAPTER 20

The Importance of Self-Worth

You are not a drop in the ocean.
You are the entire ocean in a drop.
— Rumi

Looking In isn't just about who we think we are — it's also about the model we're using to define ourselves. It includes how we feel about our worth and value. Our experiences often reflect and reveal the identity we've accepted — and whether we believe we're worthy of love, purpose, and divine guidance. If we notice a sense of unworthiness shaping our response to a situation, we can pause and ask ourselves: What would I do differently next time?

To know yourself and take 100 percent responsibility for what you think about yourself is, for many, a lifelong pursuit and one that often remains incomplete by the time we pop off the planet. It's not surprising then that religion, theology, mysticism, philosophy, reason, science, and everything in between have something to say about knowing the self.

Even if we are not philosophical or spiritual in our approach to understanding self, when quantum physics acknowledges through the observer effect that what you focus on directly affects your experience, we are prompted on a deep level to take seriously the efforts to know ourselves. The way in which we identify ourselves is seen clearly in the evidence of our experience.

Over many years, I've learned the hard way that truly knowing myself requires departing from the sense of self that is based on how other people treat me or see me. Personality, ego, accumulation of external identifiers, status, acknowledgements, and other external influences have actually been distractions that keep me away from knowing my true self based in the sacred and divine. This idea is echoed in collective wisdom: "Know thyself," "To thine own self be true," and "The kingdom of God is within you." Choose your flavor and find it voiced in a way that suits you. Bottom line: To truly know yourself, you must go within and discover what is held in consciousness.

In my twenties, the outside shaped the inside rather than the inside shaping the outside. I looked at what I was doing to identify who I was, rather than knowing who I was and then looking out to see the effortless expression of what I knew myself to be. We might think of it like this: am I running to stay in shape, or am I running because I'm in shape? Am I in an experience to shape who I am, or am I in an experience because of who I am?

Back then, I lived and worked in Boston as a television producer at *The Monitor Channel*. My stomping grounds were the best Back Bay had to offer — shopping, movie theaters, restaurants. I would stride confidently through Copley Place, Boston's newly-developed upscale shopping venue, the well-marbled floor accentuating the click of my Bruno Mali three-inch leather pumps. It felt good to be a young professional with independence, a strong sense of purpose, and passion for my work as a news producer and anchor. I look back now and see how my self-esteem was bolstered by my success, which the world deemed worthy of applause. I felt good about my achievements and sincerely Looked Up to listen for divine guidance, but I was still identifying myself based on what I did for work and how it made me look to others.

My daily rhythm was fast and focused. Keeping up with news and production deadlines and life in the city demanded it. One day, strutting through Copley Place, I saw three guys walking abreast, the one on the right carrying a massive boombox on his shoulder, blasting "Black or White" by Michael Jackson. I veered slightly to get around them just as he turned to talk to his friend. The boombox swung right at my head. I instinctively leaned away to avoid the collision.

"Whoa," I muttered to myself, grateful it hadn't smashed my face. I walked on, thinking nothing of it and headed for the down escalator, which would take me across a glass bridge towards my condo.

Halfway down, BOOM . . . he smashed the boombox on my head. Full force. I didn't know they'd caught up and were standing right behind me.

Stay conscious! was all I could manage to think. Surprise, shock, and pain laser focused my attention. *Don't pass out on the escalator!* I grabbed the handrail. *Don't fall down. You'll get chewed by the escalator teeth!*

The three guys laughed, pushed past, and raced to the next escalator with an exit onto Huntington Avenue. I stabilized myself, completely dazed and in pain. A security guard sat at a mini kiosk between the two escalators.

"They just attacked me," I said to him shakily. In a feeble attempt to be heard and seen, I pointed to the guys now exiting the building.

He was oblivious, calmly perched on his stool, slightly slumped over to read his paperback held in one hand. The conclusion of this flash assessment? He hadn't seen anything and there was no point to engage. I realized any resolution was on me and made a decision to follow them. The guard barely looked up as I grabbed the rail of the second escalator to steady myself and follow them as best I could while in pain and mental fog. I tracked them as they laughed and joked, and made their way over to a nearby intersection. I didn't want them to see me and come after me again. My stumbling pace put a safe distance between us. Miraculously, a police car pulled up just as I approached the intersection where they stood facing the other direction. I quickly explained the assault and pointed them out to the police just as they turned around, saw us, and descended the Boylston Street subway entrance. The cops looked up and watched them disappear.

"They're gone now, and there's no way to catch them," the police said. I listened with a dazed stare, adrenaline now wearing off. I knew I had a bit of a walk to get home.

"Do you want us to call an ambulance?"

"No, thank you." My auto response overrode the moment. I had the tools I needed to handle what was in front of me, but I also didn't really consider what had just happened in making the decision. It didn't really occur to me to ask for help or accept help when it was offered. I was used to handling problems and knew from experience that others' assessments based on external evidence ultimately gave me more to deal with and overcome. I immediately responded in my own thought. The internal dialog was like two lawyers arguing before a judge. It went something like this.

"I just got assaulted and smashed in the head. It hurts," presenting the material evidence. "If you claim the assault, you also claim all the effects from the assault. Whatever is held in thought will be reflected in experience. You are a victim. They attacked you." The physical facts screamed in my head.

"We are both children of God and innocent. This violence is an imposition on me and on them. This incident isn't based on their true self either. When thinking clearly, they wouldn't do this. I don't need to attach the label of attacker to them anymore than I want to attach the label of victim to me."

This is where the fork in the road becomes critical, and the choice alters what comes next.

"You feel faint and have a long walk home. How are you going to get there?" Physical evidence argues its case to get me to take it on as the prominent thought of myself.

If I take into thought that I've just been assaulted and dwell on that as the reality of my being, I open myself up to all the resultant pain and timeline of recovery. If I hold in thought the reality of my spiritual identity as being untouched by circumstances, I can more quickly see and realize it. Do I admit my own inability to handle this, ask God for help, and experience the divine power? Or do I manage it myself as my own problem, call it mine, and deal with all the effects of it, and resort to positive thinking as my mind over matter?

"Lisa, you have a choice. Will you argue on the side of the problem or ask for grace in the moment to shift your heart and work towards healing?"

If I sink into self-pity or identify myself as a victim, I will certainly feel all the effects of that identification. But if I identify myself as God identifies me and not take on the identity of the victim, if I feel love instead of anger or fear, if I choose to identify the assailants as God identifies them and not see them as attackers, we are all free from the false identification and the results thereof.

I was able to forgive them right away when I realized their horrible behavior didn't stem from who they truly were. By forgiving them immediately, I was freed to see my real identity as God's child. This view was not predicated on an external change. In fact, claiming my true identity, as well as theirs, sped the process of seeing the truth.

This reasoned approach supported me as I slowly walked the five blocks home. I honestly don't remember the walk very well. I do remember the head pain and nausea, what I now know to be symptoms of concussion.

When I got home, the one thought that brought clarity and freedom from pain was that no material circumstance, no matter how disturbing or jarring, could touch who I was as God's child, nor could anything change my love for God or God's love for me. When I felt God's love for me, I didn't feel the pain. I still hadn't completely let go of feeling like I was vulnerable to attack. I had gotten clear on my identity and overcome the pain, but I had not dealt with the bigger idea of random violence as a lingering possibility.

The next day, I was back at work as the producer of the daily TV news program *Today's Monitor*, which presented on television the international daily newspaper, *The Christian Science Monitor*. It was shot smack dab in the middle of the atmospheric, bustling newsroom, the perfect backdrop for the show. Our on-location control room was set up out of the way against a wall. I sat facing the bank of monitors, headset on, with my back to the set and the rest of the newsroom. The path for employees going in or out of the newsroom ran right behind me.

Most of the writers, editors, and staff initially rejected the idea of a TV show about the paper — let alone a set in the middle of the newsroom — believing it would be too disruptive and distracting to their work or discourage people from reading the paper. They, like most newspapers, were fighting a declining audience as it was. It took a while for the newsroom to embrace the concept and changes to their normal routines, but the audience loved the show, and it brought more attention to the Pulitzer Prize-winning newspaper and its long history of excellence in journalism, which was ultimately the goal. One particularly strident holdout to the new concept — the famous cartoonist — had a reputation for volatility and was none too pleased to see his cartoon represented on television. He abhorred the idea and made that very clear to the editor. The compromise was that we would simply show the image of his cartoon on the screen while an anchor read his caption. No commentary, no interpretation. It was the last segment of the show before the anchors would wrap up and sign off.

Because we were in the newsroom, we ran the show with a skeletal crew and without an associate producer. I was responsible for back-timing the show and making sure I knew exactly how many seconds were left for the anchors to sign off before the credit roll. We could run credits faster or slower as a buffer, but I had to be very precise. I love math and was generally very good at calculating in base six what was needed, and it was faster to do it in my head on the fly than use a time calculator. But this particular day, the numbers were all a blur, and it hurt to think and calculate. It wasn't commonly known back then that concussions affected processing and concentration.

That issue became moot very quickly. The cartoonist overheard the anchors introduce his cartoon. He bolted out of his office in a rage about his cartoon on TV. Meanwhile, I was consumed by calculating under pressure, concentrating on the anchors to give them the needed countdown.

The next moment is seared in memory. The cartoonist, holding a massive hardcover book of archived cartoons, stopped behind me, turned, and smashed the book on the crown of my head in exactly the same place I'd been hit the day before by the boombox. Instant tears welled up from the pain. I went down, collapsing on the narrow bit of counter in front of the bank of monitors and controls. He hit me so hard that the loud thwack of the book on my skull completely stopped the newsroom.

Everything went silent. Everyone looked up from what they were doing and turned towards the sound. But because I had collapsed on the desk out of view, nobody saw anything unusual. Content that he made his statement loud and clear, the cartoonist stormed back to his office, and everyone went back to what they were doing.

I managed the pain and ended the show. I did nothing else in response. I didn't tell the editor or confront the cartoonist. I just wanted to disappear. I felt embarrassed to have disrupted the newsroom, and because it had taken so long for our show to gain some level of acceptance, I didn't want to ruffle feathers. I was probably in shock and not thinking clearly, but even afterwards, I didn't speak up.

In an attempt to keep the external peace, I diminished my own needs, told the crew I was okay, and went on with the show. I denied my own value to be sure everyone else was comfortable and didn't take a stand against the wrong that had been done. I gave the impression that everything was fine, when in fact, it wasn't. I was in pain and had a compound concussion. Though I got past the pain, I didn't address the lack of self-worth and lack of self-awareness at the root of my reluctance to face the problem.

Our choices don't change who we are,
they only change our experience.

Making the outside picture look good for the sake of image is not what this book is about on any level. When we do that, it tends to not go well. The whole point of this book is to show that we must align our thought of ourselves with who we truly are spiritually, and in doing so, we see the outside picture reflect that deeper knowing and alignment.

Both these experiences highlighted a victim mentality that needed to be seen and rooted out of my concept of self. Each experience we have gives us the opportunity to examine thought and how we view ourselves. Do we allow our self-concept to be shaped by how others see us or treat us?

We never need to feel like a victim or powerless, but circumstances often scream this as our reality. What we do in that instant is all important. We must know that our identity does not stem from outward experience. When you choose how you identify yourself, this will ultimately govern your experience. Our choices don't change who we are, they only change our experience.

If you identify in the moment as a victim or as powerless in the face of an outward circumstance, it will not lead to a solution. You will achieve the opposite — you cave in on yourself; you don't seek help, reach out for support, or look for a way out.

To identify yourself as a victor — powerful and worthy of love simply because you exist — helps you realize that any other kind of treatment is unacceptable. Identifying yourself rightly gives you the strength to take a stand for what is right.

When we feel the humility and courage to Look Up and call on God, the grace of God is present, even in circumstances that try to tell us love doesn't exist. God is everywhere and all-powerful. God is always available. And when we turn to God, Love, we open the door for the Holy Spirit to enter into the moment and transform our experience. The power of God, Christ, reveals in our thought the perfect idea of us, pure and true. God is good and expressed as you. We are created for a reason, with a purpose, and when we accept that, the "peace of God that passes all understanding," opens our eyes to the gift we've been given.

Side note — Right after I edited these two stories of getting my head bashed, I was cleaning up the kitchen with my husband. I needed a container from the bottom drawer, bent down to open the drawer, and asked him to step a bit to the side so I could pull it out. He did, and continued doing what he was doing in the cabinet above me and then walked over to the fridge. I found the container and top I needed and stood up. I royally smashed my head, in exactly the same place, on the upper cabinet door he'd left open.

He doesn't leave cabinets open. I don't bash my head. Coincidence? What we hold in thought, we see in our experience. Be alert to what you hold in thought.

Looking In, taking responsibility for our thought of ourselves, demands discipline. It takes practice. Be mindful of the self-talk, positive or negative, identifying us as either powerful manifestations of Life or out of control reactions to circumstance and feelings. We get to choose. Look Up to know the Source. Look In to identify yourself based on that Source and remain unswayed by external evidence or sensation. Once you recognize that the external is the outward manifestation of thought, you won't look to it as the cause of experience. You'll handle issues at their source, in consciousness. And the degree to which you realize that your mind is the manifestation of God, Mind, your thought will be clear and free from false beliefs of another source.

CHAPTER 21

Know What's Right for You

The question, "Do I feel happy about this?" is not a frivolous one.
— Alex Noble

When we're young, we have an undeniable sense of self — we know our heart and preferences. As we grow up and get distracted by societal or familial expectations and thoughts of who we're supposed to be, we often lose sight of the simplicity of just being ourselves — effortless, pure, and free. When we catch a glimpse of this knowing as adults, we remember who we are. It is a sense of fullness that comes from within, not from without. It is an inherent knowing, a gift from the Creator. Sometimes, a place, a smell, or sound, a memory or a person calls us back to that clear and innocent sense of being ourselves.

For me, this place of being is found in my love of the ocean and the sound of seagulls, a desire to be alone and hear the water flow over rocks, feeling completely myself in those beat-up jeans or boots, or my smile, which I know comes from my love for God — a deep reverence and gratitude for life and all things spiritual. Those moments feel magical and pure and spark a desire, "I'd like more of that, please." The real trick is to act when we feel this clarity and watch our experience flow out of this way of being with ease. Our experience becomes a reflection of our clear sense of self. The fullness gets reflected back to us in magical ways.

On a particularly cool November day in Boston, I was overtaken by a powerful urge to go windsurfing. It was overcast and a bit foggy, the breeze steady but not very strong. Definitely not ideal conditions.

It's cold and foggy, I argued. *The wind is too low to really sail. Why would you get all geared up for these conditions? It's too much effort.*

I rationalized and discarded the thought. And then I remembered what used to happen to me as a child, when the experience of knowing would guide me to action. It used to happen a lot when I was around seven or eight. I would wake up and feel in my bones that I needed to be alone — not play with the neighborhood kids, not hang out with my mom or siblings, not fulfill someone else's desire for me to do something. I would know beyond a doubt that I yearned to be quiet and felt called into nature.

My "special place," as I deemed it, was a small babbling brook in the middle of the forest, which happened to be on the far side of a swamp. On days when I needed to be alone, I'd let my mom know I was going to my "special place" and venture off in shorts and a T-shirt and bare feet in my Keds, ride my bike to the edge of the wood, and then island-hop through the swamp, to avoid falling in and soggy, swamp-mud sneakers.

I yearned for the time to mentally float, and with nature as the backdrop, let my thoughts drift. I anticipated the calming sound of water, the gentle pock, pock, gurgle of the brook over and around the stones. I would stay there for hours, not thinking about people or chores, hunger pangs, or needing to be home at a certain time. As the brook flowed, I flowed with deep knowing. I didn't think about it; I was guided and governed without effort. Then there would come a moment when it was time to leave. I felt it. It came when I felt full and ready to re-enter my life as I knew it.

Those days always satisfied and deeply enriched me. They confirmed who I was. I didn't need anything from anyone or anything. My life was complete. Magical moments of oneness always occurred during these adventures. Communing with nature and talking with trees and rocks and water felt natural. There was an understanding that surpassed words.

As adults, we often forget these moments. We forget how easy it was as children to let go and feel guided. Back on that chilly November day in Boston, the recollection of my childhood experiences hit me in a flash while I stood in my Back Bay condo, arguing with the urge to go windsurfing. I needed to heed the urge.

The decision made, I walked to the garage, hopped into my silver Mazda GLC with two boards on top, sails, boom, and gear in the back, and headed to Pleasure Bay in the heart of South Boston, my regular windsurfing destination.

My board rigged, I donned my full wetsuit with a strong conviction to stay on my board and out of the icy water. I *put in* by the strip of beach on the south side of the breakwater. I stepped onto my board, barely touching the water long enough to feel the cold, and sailed away from the shore. There was a stillness on the water. Salt water and salt air felt like home to me. I sailed parallel about thirty yards out from the shore through the mist, listening to the water gently slap the board. It was a gentle sail, no need for effort, the weight of the sail and my body balanced and steady. Not long after I'd been out on the water, the most magical thing happened. I heard bagpipes. I thought I was imagining it, but sure enough, I saw a gentleman walking the beach in the cold mist, playing his bagpipes.

The sound lilted over the water and swirled around me, carried on the wind. I was enveloped in the magic of the moment. Time stopped. This captured my essence. All the elements of the experience came together, and my whole being felt complete. It was what I used to feel when I knew it was time to leave my "special place" as a kid, filled up and at one with Life.

"Do I feel happy about this? Does this bring me peace?" are not frivolous questions.

This experience telegraphs something very important. When we follow our intuition, that still small voice within, even in the face of reason and common sense, we find our way to synchronicities and magic, and all that is meant for us appears in our experience. If we resist these promptings, it's not that something bad will happen, necessarily, but we postpone an opportunity to come into alignment with who we are, a fuller sense of ourselves, undistracted by externals, and we can miss the expression of that alignment showing up in our lives.

Why was I prompted to go windsurfing just at that moment? Why did the bagpiper decide to go play on the beach that day in the cold mist? Why did I decide to windsurf outside the bay when I'd always windsurfed inside the breakwater? Why did I sail along the beach instead of straight out into the channel? Why did all those little nudges guide me to hear and see him play? The questions distract us from the point. When I followed my intuition, my experience lined up with my heart, with who I knew myself to be deep down inside, with the core of me, with the place in me that feels like home, safety, and full expression without judgment, and my experience reflected all of it.

To Look Up and listen. To Look In and affirm our identity. To Look Out and see it confirmed. Here's another way of articulating this:

- Discern the lens you look through.

- Affirm the identity you claim.

- Confirm the evidence you seek.

EXERCISE

Reflect for a moment on your own special place. This may be a place, a feeling, an imagination, a person living or dead, a song, a poem, an activity. The possibilities are endless.

- Where is it? Or ask who, what, when is it?

- What does it evoke inside of you?

- What part of you does it resonate with?

- Does this place shift you at your core?

- Does it make you come alive or feel more alive?

- Does it connect you to All that is?

This exercise is to wake you up to your deepest alignment. What bridges the inside and outside and speaks the language of your soul's desire? Allow yourself to listen to your heart and ask what would make you deeply at peace and happy. "Do I feel happy about this? Does this bring me peace?" are not frivolous questions.

Trust and Let Go

My whole life has been about letting go of control. So it's fitting that this book's culminating stories cover this overarching topic: letting go of control and yielding to the divine. Let's sincerely ask ourselves, is every protracted challenge we face simply the reflection of a place in us that is unwilling to let go of control? I ask the question, "Where can I let go of control?" more quickly now because it's taken me so many failed attempts to understand and so many years of struggle before I was willing to yield. Now I'm much more willing to notice a desire to control. If I find myself trying to control what's out there, I pivot and choose to Look In and ask how my view needs to shift. Where can I let go of control? I Look Up and ask, how can I acknowledge God's control, align with the All-power, and get out of the way?

Look Up, Look In, Look Out applied in reverse order, when there's a problem, is a powerful tool that supports me every time. If there's a problem out there, I Look In to check if I'm thinking accurately within myself. And if there's any uncertainty in that area, I Look Up to realign my thought with the divine and true. Having this simple, effective framework means that whenever there's trouble "out there," I know what to do to find the solution.

In the following chapters, I will share stories that demonstrate how hard it was for me to let go. I learned the hard way. I struggled mightily to let go. I will share examples of letting go of control and outlining outcomes in work, parenting, being a daughter, my purpose, and ultimately in being myself. Stay with me through the weeds of this because you may be facing some or all of these issues yourself, and I'd love to offer you examples of what it looks like to use these tools over the arc of years, telescoped into a few stories.

CHAPTER 22

Follow Your Convictions

Your decisions will master you, whichever direction they take.
— Mary Baker Eddy

My mom and I trekked into Boston in her yellow AMC Hornet on a frigid January evening to see the off-Broadway production of *Godspell* at the Wilbur Theater on Tremont Street. It was a big deal for me. Transfixed by the performance, I felt a conviction. I knew without a doubt I'd be in *Godspell* someday. I had no real reason to think this — no evidence to support my conviction — but the certainty was solid as concrete.

The theater bug had bitten me at Meadowcroft Summer Day Camp at the age of five when I was cast in my first leading role as Christopher Robin in "In which Christopher Robin Leads an Expotition to the North Pole." My obsession grew along with me, fueled by years of school musicals and community theater.

By the summer of '76, before my senior year, I had visions of the Broadway stage. I played the 33 rpm vinyl album of the Broadway cast recording of *Godspell* on my mint green plastic record player with a built-in speaker. With every lyric committed to memory, I belted out one song after another as the needle grooved deeper into the vinyl. My mom, thankfully, never complained or hinted at tiring of it. With the bedroom my own, my sister gone on a bike trek to Maine, I practiced performing in front of an audience, confidently gesturing to the glass-eyed menagerie of stuffed animals on my bed.

News traveled fast in Cohasset. The drama department was holding auditions for the fall musical the first week in August. The show, *Godspell*.

This was it! My vision would be realized. I imagined singing, "Where Are You Going" as I raced my brother's blue '68 convertible Camaro to the high school to read all the details posted outside the auditorium. Then my heart sank. The date of the audition was the same day the Greyhound bus left for the Adventure Unlimited Ranches (A/U) summer camp in Colorado. I'd spent all summer working to pay for it: painting house interiors, babysitting, and ushering and managing a concession stand at the South Shore Music Circus. After my parents' divorce, aside from Mom's once-a-year school-clothes purchase, I paid for my own clothes and any extras I wanted — records, JJ's ice cream after the Sailing Club races, and summer camp. I never minded paying for things. Daddy started us saving money at a very young age.

The money I'd saved all summer was just enough to pay for camp. I spent it all; it meant that much to me. This was my fourth summer at A/U. The programs were designed to empower young people to demonstrate a reliance on God, choosing faith over fear in challenging outdoor activities: technical rock climbing, horseback riding, whitewater rafting, mountain climbing, pushing our limits physically and socially. We proved our faith by our actions. I loved being in an atmosphere where fearless reliance on God wasn't questioned, criticized, or bullied into silence, but rather expected, applauded, and encouraged as a way of thinking and being that shaped action. As much as I desperately wanted to be in *Godspell*, I didn't want to miss going to camp.

Even though the departure schedule made it obvious I'd miss the audition, I felt an odd calm about it. I knew something would work out. Both ideas felt aligned with who I was. Being the fullest expression of me was the whole point of being on the planet. How could Life squash its own expression? This was my thought process and what I claimed. This was my version of Looking Up at the time — trusting in an order larger than what my eyes or reason could see and being willing to let go of my own outline of what was right for me.

The day of the audition, ready with bags packed for camp, I had an extra ten minutes before we needed to meet the bus. The school auditorium was on the way out of town. Since I hadn't planned to audition, I didn't remember what time they started, but I asked my mom to swing by just in case someone was there.

The director was setting up. A few students were there waiting for things to start.

"Hi Mr. Emmonds."

"Auditions will begin in a half hour."

I told him I wanted more than anything to be in the show but only had minutes before I needed to catch a bus to Colorado and would be at camp for the next three weeks. He seemed glad to see my enthusiasm and asked me to sing two songs.

I wasn't nervous. I'd sung the songs all summer. I sat downstage left on the front edge, hands curled around the lip of the wood stage on either side of my legs, feet dangling. One song felt good. The other song, sung by a guy on the album, felt low and out of my range. He asked me to sing it high. Having belted out songs all summer, I felt more awkward than confident singing softly in my upper register, though the director seemed pleased.

Though I'd had a conviction that I'd be in *Godspell* someday after seeing the performance in Boston, I didn't outline when or how I'd be in the show and wasn't attached to anything except the idea. I thought through a version of what's now Look Up, Look In, Look Out. I acknowledged Life is always fully expressed, and that as a reflection or manifestation of Life, my expression couldn't be limited. It was in Life's best interest for me to have experiences that highlighted my individuality and expression. I trusted that if it was right for me, it would be in my experience, and I let it go. When I learned of the timing conflict of the auditions for the high school production, I put it in God's hands and released my attachment to being in it. So after the audition, I quickly moved off the negative feelings that I hadn't done my best or wouldn't get a part and instead called it good, happy to have sung and dipped my toe in the musical theater process.

When I returned from camp three weeks later, we drove by the school to see the cast list posted in the glass case by the doors of the auditorium.

Jesus — Lisa T.

Judas — Nancy T.

John — Eric J.

Mary Magdalene — Margaret B.

The list went on . . .

Playing Jesus in *Godspell* — memorizing the book of Matthew as the script and acting out the life of the man I'd grown up knowing as "the most scientific man who ever trod the globe," as described in *Science and Health* — humbled me. He lived by the laws of God, the laws of good — the very laws I'd been studying and striving to demonstrate since childhood. It all solidified something in me. I felt uniquely fashioned for this role. It was the highest role I could imagine playing.

The show was so popular, we were asked to extend our run another week. Somehow the word had spread, and people even came down from Boston to see our little high school production. I do have to hand it to our Director Ron Emmonds, who decided to cast women for the two male leads. This wasn't out of a lack of men but an artistic choice. Or perhaps, something larger than all of us was governing, and it was meant to be.

The whole experience became a confirmation of my heart and what I loved. I spoke to audiences the words Jesus spoke to his disciples. The last performance was an out-of-body experience for me. I remember my opening line and then the audience applauding. Everything in between was a blank. It's as though I wasn't there performing as a high school senior who loved theater, but for those two hours, I was living as Jesus himself. It was a true experience of letting go of self and being someone bigger, the best and truest of life. For a few hours, my experience was the embodiment of all the spiritual understanding of my seventeen-year-old awareness.

Letting go of my own sense of self that night left an indelible impression on me. Looking Up and knowing true Self, Looking In and seeing only that reflection since that was the role I was playing, allowed me to Look Out and actually experience the true Self. I felt the fullness of Jesus' words, "I and my Father are one." That stays with me to this day.

The point of this is not for you to rush out and find a production of *Godspell* or play the role of Jesus; it's to know that you can mentally do the same thing. Know the highest Self (Look Up), let go of a limited self-concept (Look In and let go of false limiting beliefs and embrace the unlimited good of who you are), and then embody and express the good (Look Out).

Anyone can take the steps and move forward in this way. It is a simple process, but that doesn't mean it's always easy. I've failed more times than I can count. But the key is to practice, to repeat the process so many times that it becomes a habit. Even if you fail each attempt, keep going! Because at some point, you'll succeed, and when that moment comes, it's the start of a new life for you. Then you've proven to yourself that you can be who you've always known yourself to be on the inside.

We cannot take control of our life until we take control of our choices.

Deep down, we all feel a yearning, no matter which cards we were dealt. Were we challenged or coddled? Did we experience abuse or praise? Violence or comfort? Poverty or riches? Lack or abundance? High expectations or no expectations? An emphasis on education or not? Good role models or bad? It doesn't matter. Each and every one of us feels a yearning, a certainty deep down that we are unique and special and meant for more. The strength of that flame, which is sometimes the tiniest spark, is up to you. Until we take full responsibility for our own flame inside, we will not live the life we were meant to live. If we blame our past, the people (or lack thereof) in our lives, our circumstances, externals of all kinds, then we will be stuck in life framed by limits, forever struggling against elements out of our control.

We cannot take control of our life until we take control of our choices. But when we realize that, we determine our future and the quality of our life by the choices we make. Wait a second, didn't you just tell us to *let go* a few paragraphs ago? Yes. So here's the hitch. We need to take control of two choices — first, we must choose if the source of reality and power is internal or external, and second, choose if the source of our identity is the small egoic self filled with limitation or the divine infinite Self, expansive and limitless. When we Look Up to the one divine Self and then Look In to our true self as a reflection of the divine Self, we can then Look Out and see our true self and everyone else's true self expressed. This Up-In-Out way of thinking is what let the *Godspell* and camp experiences flow the way they did.

This is where the letting go comes in. When we choose to let go of the small self and opt for the big Self, the struggle drops away. We find the ease of expression that includes all the power of the Infinite. The struggle comes from the small self's desire to hang on, outline, control, fight, find excuses, be the victim, have a justification for things not working out. These feelings are intimate to all of us on some level. We've all experienced the pain of not letting go of something. The pain comes more from the struggle to let go than it does from the dashed expectation. One of my favorite quotes about this is from Kyle Cease, "They didn't break your heart; they broke your expectations."

So letting go of little self is a big step and often a hard-won victory in the moment, but these wins are an ongoing process, an infinite game as James P. Carse would say, and often involve facing down fears of loss and abandonment. The little self doesn't like being denied and you can expect it will tempt you into playing small, staying comfortable, and returning to the familiar, even when the familiar is limiting, fearsome, and at times dangerous. It takes practice. Failed attempts transform into small wins, and then consistent wins, and eventually success at letting go becomes the rhythm of life — but only if you keep practicing, choosing, and choosing again. Choose to let go of external validation, egoic control, small self, and doingness. Choose divine Self, internal knowing, Ego's control, and being the reflection of the All. This choice matters over and over again.

✦ CHAPTER 23 ✦

Trust Life to Align Supply and Demand

God shall supply all your need according to his riches in glory.
— Philippians 4:19

The power of Life aligns need and supply. This power is Spirit and is always available to us. This first occurs in the realm of ideas and then is seen in experience.

The need for shelter is something we all share. How we go about finding housing varies as much as our individual natures. The approach we take is often based on the law of supply and demand, and more often than not, the demand is greater than the supply. This leads to a scarcity mindset and competition.

The abundance mentality focuses on the fact that there's a right place for each of us. The place we seek is seeking us. There's a governing force aligning those seeking with those offering, and this power is always available to us in thought. The abundance mindset focuses on qualities and ideas rather than things. Each person's home consists of or expresses spiritual qualities — light, flow, balance, feeling of place, freedom, peace, safety, and so forth — always available to everyone in limitless supply because they're spiritual ideas.

When we recognize that we already include the qualities we like and want more of, we know we could never lack them in our experience. Their expression is not dependent on first finding them externally because they exist already within us. As I recognize the expression of these qualities in myself, I more quickly recognize them expressed in my experience. This happens when you buy a new car and then see that type of car everywhere you go, whereas before you didn't see them. Were they not there or did you just not see them?

Neuroscience confirms that the RAS (reticular activating system) will seek evidence of what we affirm as true — it filters the information to show us what we want to see. So why not use that to your advantage? Don't wait to see the evidence; affirm it before you see it. By affirming good and the desires of your heart, you will see more evidence of both, and the good in your life will grow.

Does this mean the good wasn't there before and you're creating it by affirming it? No. It means you see more of the reality of goodness that has always been there. You know that line "I was blind and now I see?" That takes on a different ring when you understand that what we now see has always been there; it was only the shades of doubt and fear that had previously hidden it from view. The divine reality of all good is what is seen when a limited sense of reality is dropped. We can choose to see beyond a limited material sense of reality or even a quantum sense of reality and accept the divine reality. Wayne Dyer said it very simply, "When you change the way you look at things, the things you look at change."

The same principle is operating when we deal with finding a place to live. As consciousness holds the idea, it is seen in experience. This is scientific and can be understood as a form of quantum entanglement. Bottom line, the more I acknowledge that I already include the qualities I seek to see in a place — light, flow, balance, coziness, freedom, peace, safety, etc. — the more quickly I will see in my experience the place that expresses those qualities.

Each apartment and house I've lived in has its own story — how I was led to it by the voice within rather than by the statistics and data of the day. The places have changed, but the process has remained the same.

Looking for my first apartment in Boston in 1982 started as most searches did then, by putting the word out and looking in newspapers. When nothing jumped out as the winner, it became a lose-lose battle to stop the bleeding of cash. What could I find that wouldn't bleed my savings dry, that was livable, and didn't include too many city-dwelling red flags — roaches, rats, noise, or lack of safety. The external approach quickly exposed itself as a losing proposition. This approach focused on what I didn't want instead of what I did, on lack instead of abundance, and on all the externals as governing my experience instead of bringing my thought into alignment with what was already present.

I turned upward and inward. I looked at the list of physical requirements I'd made for my new place and translated those into spiritual qualities. A one-bedroom became privacy and coziness, high ceilings became spaciousness, windows became light, well-patrolled neighborhood became safety, good room layout became flow and fluidity, and quiet became peace. The conversation about price became a conversation about value and worthiness. What I could *get* for the money based on an apartment's value became what I could *give* based on my value, sense of worthiness, and the qualities I expressed.

I knew that the spiritual qualities of light and safety, beauty and harmony, space and peace, and alignment of place were all in abundant supply. Ideas are unlimited. Everyone in existence could think of the number three at the same time, and we'd never run out of threes. It's an idea and therefore not constrained by matter. So the spiritual qualities that would be available to me were also unlimited. This freed me from thinking in a limited way about where this apartment would appear and how much it would cost. If these ideas were included in my thought, they had to appear in my experience. This approach opened up possibilities for me.

When I started looking for spiritual qualities in my search, I found them everywhere and very quickly dropped the limited mindset of scarcity and lack. I spent my days feeling grateful for the abundance of qualities I could see expressed all around me. I noticed an arrangement on the table that expressed beauty and peace, saw the sunlight fill the room that uplifted my spirit, felt the space around me that flowed with me, or felt satisfied with just enough food. I knew that my concept of housing would find expression when I felt it was true to my way of being.

I was living with my mom in Kingston at the time on the south shore of Boston and commuting every day very early in the morning. I longed to be in the city and walk to work. I remained patient and diligent, focusing on expressing the qualities I desired to see more of in my life and particularly in an apartment. I included all the ideas within me and didn't need to look outside of me to feel abundant or whole.

I kept an eye out and still asked people if they knew of anything. Nothing seemed to be appearing. I'd taken all the human footsteps to find a place and finally gave up. I Looked Up and turned the whole thing over to the law of good. There had to be a solution. I got very still and Looked In — reaffirmed that I included, right here and right now, every good quality and the expression of those qualities. And I Looked Out — I trusted the law to be operating in my experience regardless of the lack of evidence.

Our experience is the expression or manifestation of our thoughts, not the other way around.

In a few minutes, the phone rang. It was a girl I didn't know very well. We'd crossed paths a few years back in a youth group. She said, "You came to mind, and I wanted to call and ask if you'd be interested in my apartment. My roommate is leaving, and we could share the apartment for a few months before I leave. Then it will be yours."

Her apartment was the top floor of an old four-story brownstone that stood alone (the Midtown Hotel had been built around it, covering the rest of the block). It had hardwood parquet floors, ten-foot ceilings with turn-of-the-century crown moldings, solid mahogany pocket doors that divided the living room and bedroom, and there was a roof deck!

"Oh, and by the way," she continued, "it's under rent control, so with your name on the lease while we share it, the rent won't go up when I leave in a few months."

It was a third of other rents in the area. And where was it located? Directly across the street from where I worked! I could actually see the building I worked in from the bay window in the living room. I knew it was right and said yes, sight unseen. I lived there for years, saving up enough money to buy my first condo before passing it along to a dear musician friend who needed an affordable place near Berklee School of Music.

EXERCISE

Note that in the above situation, the answer came very quickly when I took three distinct steps. Here's an exercise to lead you through the same steps.

Step one: Get clear about what you want. It's okay to start with a list of physical things you want in a home. Then your task is to exchange the physical things for ideas and qualities. Ask yourself, "What does this physical thing on my list represent spiritually?" and write down the spiritual quality that you see expressed in the material condition you listed.

Step two: Acknowledge the infinite nature of Spirit and the infinite nature of spiritual qualities. Acknowledge God, Spirit, as the source. Acknowledge that as a reflection of God made in His image, these qualities are already inside of you, a part of who you are. *The Kingdom of Heaven is within you.* You manifest these qualities; think about them, express them, feel them, be grateful for them, embrace them as qualities you care about, notice them being expressed in various ways around you. Become very aware of these spiritual qualities in your current, present experience.

Step three: Let go of outlining what the result must look like and trust that the Force — the Power governing all of creation and holding everything in perfect order and balance — supports you. This power is seen operating as Alignment, Expression, Abundance, Truth, Adjustment, Balance, Progress, and Love — all working in harmony to bring the spiritual qualities you hold dear into expression. Every spiritual principle based on the law of God or law of good is working in your favor to bring to the surface, into your present, conscious awareness, the effect of this law. Since the law of good is always operating, more good is always available, so when we yield to this law, we see more good in our experience. In other words, you can expect to see or find the collection of qualities that you listed in a home.

When we allow ourselves to yield to the principle governing right alignment, we become more aware of the ideas and impulses that lead us toward the outward manifestation of that alignment. In so doing, we can expect to see supply meet the need — in my case, finding an apartment that met my need.

Letting go of the outcome can feel awkward at first. You may think, "Don't we need to control the result? Don't we need to make it happen? Don't we need to do something?" That's the ego talking — that place in you that thinks you lack something — that place in you that thinks you need to go out and get something to fill you up. So that's where trust comes in. Trust that your identity includes all the qualities of a home. You need to trust that being and expressing those qualities will naturally cause them to appear in your experience. Our experience is the expression or manifestation of our thoughts, not the other way around.

When you don't see the evidence right away, what is your response? To think the law of good is not working? To question whether you're worthy? To sink into discouragement and accept less than? These responses are signals to Look Up, Look In, and Look Out. They mark the need for an adjustment to bring you into alignment with what is meant for you. Are you outlining and looking for only a particular outcome, or are you allowing, yielding to, and aligning with the law of good? It may be that the discomfort resulting from not seeing the good is the sign pointing to the very thing in thought that is blocking you from seeing the good already available.

God is the force aligning supply and demand. God is in control. We can bring our sense of ourselves into alignment with our true self, made in the image of God where God's control is seen. We can choose to operate within that truth or not. With everything we face, we choose to see alignment or disconnect, abundance or lack, possibilities or problems. You get to choose. Your choice will govern your experience.

✳ CHAPTER 24 ✳

Trust Life to Align Desire and Expression

*Metaphysics resolves things into thoughts,
and exchanges the objects of sense for the ideas of Soul.*
— Mary Baker Eddy

F inding my first apartment by successfully utilizing scientific prayer based on the law of God gave me confidence to follow the same process whenever I dealt with real estate. Finding housing is something we all need to do. The way we approach the process changes the experience we have. My husband and I have gone through this process nine times, each with its own circumstances and challenges, but always with the Up-In-Out Way.

J. and I drove out of Boston for the last time on January 1, 1993 in two separate cars and with walkie-talkies for communication as we drove to Los Angeles. We had arranged to rent a friend's new fixer-upper, situated directly below the iconic Hollywood sign at the top of a fire road. They said we could live there until they sold their current home and were able to start renovations. When they received an offer on their house later that year, they gave us the expected thirty days' notice, and we started looking.

I was working as a print and radio reporter for United Press International and in full rehearsal mode for a musical, so my schedule was maxed out. J. looked at everything on the market and picked the best he could find for us to view on weekends. Then one day, he got an intuition to look in the *Hollywood Reporter*, the industry rag that included a small real estate section listing homes for rent and sale. Generally, these listings targeted industry professionals who could afford high-ticket real estate. That was not us! But J. followed his intuition and picked up the recent edition at the Studio City newsstand on Ventura Boulevard. There was one house for rent, way out of our price range, that jumped off the page at him. Following his intuition and against the evidence that it was too expensive, he arranged to meet the owner.

When I got home that night after rehearsal, I found J. waiting up, which was unusual, and bursting to tell me something.

"The owner of that *Hollywood Reporter* house is great! She's a film costumer. She and I hit it off and talked about the industry, we both lived in NYC at the same time, and we even knew some of the same people. I told her I loved it and had to show my wife. It's amazing, really special. You have to see it!"

Walking onto the property the first time, I, too, was immediately captivated by the magic and the feel of it, just as J. had described. It had an oversized yard, fenced in for privacy, with three old-growth pine trees. And even though it was in the heart of Sherman Oaks and one block from the 101 Freeway, it was quiet and filled with light and nature. Once inside the gate, you'd never know you were in Los Angeles.

"This used to be owned by Joanna Carson," Annie told us, "who would loan it out to Truman Capote for a writing hide-away."

We effused about how much we loved the property's seclusion and peace, and that the quaint two-bedroom structure was the perfect size for us, but that unfortunately it was beyond our budget. Our only offer was to thank her for sharing her beautiful home with us.

When things feel perfect and one piece is out of place, like the price being too high, it's helpful to hold onto the thought that there must be something better. That's what we did, especially after Annie told us she was showing it to two more parties later that day. We figured it would be gone by nightfall. We let it go and kept searching, always yielding to intuition and keeping our attitude expectant.

To our surprise, it wasn't long before Annie called. "I want to rent the house to you!" she said. "I know you love the property and trust that you understand its special qualities." She offered to rent it to us for hundreds less than the listed price, even though she had several offers from renters who were ready to pay the full amount or more.

A short year later, when Annie called to say she wanted to sell it, we started looking again. The timing was not ideal to say the least; I was very pregnant with our first child. Searching produced no good results. Places were too small or too dark, not in the right area, too expensive or too loud, or too . . . we were beyond frustrated, each of us handling our frustrations on our own. It finally dawned on us to ask, "Why haven't we prayed about this together?"

We'd been praying separately all along, but hadn't sat down and thought it through together from a spiritual perspective. We listed the qualities we wanted in our home, all the qualities we'd individually been declaring as important to us when we looked for places. In the face of the evidence that there was nothing "out there," we declared that there must be a place that matched and expressed the vision of home we'd been holding in thought. We listed the qualities together.

Nothing we'd seen compared to Annie's house, but we needed to let go of outlining or holding onto any preconceived notions of what our new home would look like. Only by letting go could the qualities we loved be realized.

We decided to individually go within and listen for an amount that fairly represented what we could spend on a house. We agreed on an amount and wrote it on a piece of paper.

- We Looked Up — We acknowledged we were being guided by Life and listened for an answer.

- We Looked In — We acknowledged that our concept of home and what we valued in a home was already inside of us. We realized the solution wasn't out there; *home* was inside us, in our thought. And our concept of home would guide us to the perfect house.

- We Looked Out — We knew our experience had to align with our thought. We trusted this intuition, released the outcome, and knew the perfect house would appear.

When we claim our oneness with God, good, we see more good in our experience — we see the good idea realized as a house — a house that reflects or exhibits all the good ideas or qualities in thought. We didn't outline specifically how this spiritual concept would appear in our experience or know the next steps to take, but we trusted that we or someone else (realtor, friend, anyone on the planet), would be guided by an intuition to take action, and that those actions by whoever was prompted to take them, would lead us to alignment.

How that happens is not up to us. All we need to do is claim our oneness with the divine and be obedient to divine guidance. Simply put. Listen and follow. Trust and take action when prompted. Our experience would be aligned with the spiritual vision of our home that was held in consciousness and ultimately lead us to our home. This effect is based on the law that consciousness must be manifested, that human consciousness equals human experience.

We did what I now teach — we Looked Up to the spiritual reality of home, we Looked In to our individual concept of home, and we Looked Out and we released *how* that would be expressed outwardly in our experience. Up-In-Out.

Within a few minutes of our releasing the outcome, the phone rang. It was Annie. She told us she needed to sell her home and wanted to ask us a question.

"I know you love the house. I'm moving in with my fiancé and don't really need to make money on the deal. I just want to recoup what I owe the bank. Oh, and I have a realtor friend who can do the deal at no cost. Do you want to buy the house for what I owe the bank?"

The amount was not within thousands of the number we'd written on the paper but within hundreds! We just looked at each other. Of course it was. This was not a coincidence. It was divine alignment, supply perfectly meeting need, orchestrated by Life and not by us.

This solution resolved another concern that pressed on me while we searched for a new place to live. I was very pregnant; my due date was a month away. We could not imagine packing and moving on top of it. Now we didn't have to. We closed escrow on the house two days after our daughter was born and lived there for almost thirty years.

Our process demonstrated the practical nature of Scientific prayer, prayer based on divine law that makes the result certain. So certain, it has worked for us through many moves! It's the same divine law demonstrated by Jesus, the prophets, and in modern times by those relying on the law of God. Since praying this way is based on already-proven and demonstrated divine laws, the results are guaranteed when we live governed by divine law — *know the Truth and Truth will set you free.*

What's right isn't always easy and doesn't always follow the path of least resistance, but it does follow the path of truth affirmed and resistance released. When we follow our intuition, there may be resistance from the reasoning mind that looks through a limited lens, but there will be peace from the intuitive mind that sees reality from the standpoint of Spirit. The challenge is to release yourself from the resistance and follow the intuition in the face of reasoned resistance.

This is a key point to remember. When we release and trust that our intuition — Life — is guiding us, we need to realize that it will guide us to something that meets our needs, not necessarily our wants. We must be willing to trust that the power larger than us, divine intelligence, or the all-knowing Mind, actually knows what we need — often more accurately than we do. The question is, are we willing to let go of what we want in order to trust that our needs will be met by following our spiritual GPS (God's Positioning System)? Sometimes that takes a big leap.

Living in the San Fernando Valley for almost thirty years, we only made it to the beach a few times a year. We missed the ocean. We started talking about moving closer to the water. The process began. We listed qualities we wanted to see in our dream home. Did what we'd done each time before. Looked Up, Looked In, Looked Out. We started looking south of LA and over the course of a few years, researched properties all the way up the West Coast, California, Oregon, and Washington, finally looking in the San Juan Islands off the coast of Seattle.

The path to the house on the water took many turns. We kept allowing our steps to be governed by our expectation that all the turns in the path were aligned to reveal the best idea. We yielded to each intuition and followed each step that Life directed. We continued to look at homes coming on the market. Time passed, we stayed consistent by using our daily practices to keep us aligned with what's true instead of constantly looking at outside evidence. We affirmed and trusted we were being guided by our internal GPS, and no matter where it guided us, we would listen and follow.

Once we found the house on San Juan Island, the LA house sold in five days with seven offers, a bidding war, and a final all-cash offer way over asking price. All the details of packing and moving commenced.

Decades prior to this, I heard motivational speaker Tony Robbins say we need to commit so completely to our vision that we will "go to the island and burn the boats!" I liked the sound of that level of commitment. Hold nothing back.

I wrote in my journal, "I commit to my calling. I commit to fulfilling my life purpose. I will do whatever God wants me to do. I am here to serve. I will follow intuition no matter where it leads. I will go to the island and burn the boats!"

I thought at the time I was declaring my deep commitment, not actually committing to moving to an island or burning a boat. In the final step of our move, we packed our third U-Haul — their truck from Nova Scotia, with a picture of the Ghost Ship on the side: a square-rigger engulfed in flames. My experience reflected my commitment from years before. I was literally going to the island and burning the boat!

We need to note these moments. Record them in our hearts. Acknowledge that these are not mistakes or coincidences. They are confirmations. Evidence that what we claim for ourselves shapes our reality. This is why it is so critical to be present to and conscious of the words and intents of our heart — the unspoken thoughts deeply felt and consciously yearned for have the power to transform our experience.

To put it briefly, thoughts become things.

In quantum science, we know that the conscious thought we have must have its inevitable effect on our reality. To put it briefly, thoughts become things. What is the basis of our thought? Do we choose love or fear — internal or external — spirit or matter? If we choose the plane of spiritual reality, nothing is limited by matter and we see the effect of that awareness.

Whatever your housing scenario, you can always Look Up, Look In, and Look Out to find the place that's right for you. Places to live look like they are outside of us, but they are really just reflections of what's going on in consciousness. The laws that govern who we are as an individual are the same laws that govern what shows up in our life. What is held in consciousness as reality — what we hold as true about our identity or our home — becomes our experience, whether we want it to or not. *The onus is on us to pay attention to what is being held in consciousness as the reality.* What do you see as the reality? And how are you thinking about it? The more clearly you see that your mind is the reflection of the one divine Mind, the more your consciousness is filled with good.

The basic principle is focus on what you *want*, not on what you *don't want*. Train your thoughts and think more about what you're grateful for than about what frustrates you. Think more about what you want than about what you don't want. Hold the vision of yourself aligning with what brings you joy. See yourself living as the person you want to be and deep down inside know you are. This leaves no room for holding onto the negative thoughts that come running to your mental door. Be clear: this takes mental discipline. And also be clear that everyone has the ability to do it. This ability is anchored in the fact that your mind is a reflection of the one divine Mind, all good. Claim your oneness with the divine (Look Up), your ability to reflect the all-good of Mind (Look In), and then watch Mind be expressed as your good thinking (Look Out). At first it may feel cumbersome, but the more we practice, the better we get.

CHAPTER 25

Parenthood and Present Good

Neither shall they say, Lo here! or, lo there!
for, behold, the kingdom of God is within you.
— Luke 17:21

We got pregnant, and I started the never-ending juggling act of marriage, career, and motherhood. For anyone with children, you know how parenthood irrevocably changes your life. We had delusions of a child not changing anything. We'd hike the rainforest with the baby on our back. We'd live a life of freedom and never let a child curtail or suspend our dreams. We'd be the one set of parents who would prove that children don't need to change the life of an adult. Of course, we were dead wrong. Everything changed. And of course, we wouldn't have it any other way.

Pregnancy puts you squarely on a path of letting go of control. Women get on that path immediately; partners catch up quickly dealing with the needs of the one pregnant. A woman's body is now not fully her own; she has another purpose to serve beyond herself. And no matter how much you want to avoid the inevitable birth process, it is the freight train barreling towards you, and there's absolutely nothing you can do to stop it. The only option is to select how you want to participate in the event.

Women have been giving birth since the dawn of time, so it didn't seem this should be viewed as the medical emergency modern approaches dictate. The more I researched the birth process and attended pre-birth classes, the more natural it seemed, and the less I wanted outside procedures and requirements imposed on me or the baby. I decided to have the baby at home with a certified nurse midwife. This meant getting checked out by a doctor who deemed it safe and having a full tank of gas and the route to the hospital planned in case of an emergency. We held the expectation that all would proceed naturally and all would be well.

The path to birth was one of overcoming fear no matter where it cropped up. I'd actually had a lot of practice birthing new ideas when I was a start-up producer creating new shows for radio and TV. The process appeared the same to me: An idea grows and has its own momentum. I am a witness to the idea taking shape and form, doing all I can to stay in step with its revelation and unfoldment — while keeping ego in check and staying out of the way. Trust the process. Let go of fear. Stay out of catastrophizing. Focus on present good. Look for clues of progress. Affirm what I know to be true. Growth is a principle of life. Order is all around me expressed in nature. Proof of life is always present and ongoing. Progress is inevitable.

"Every baby comes with its own loaf of bread" was the way someone expressed it to me when fears bubbled up around whether we'd have enough income to support a child. Ideas were in infinite supply, and those ideas could be translated into action; therefore, supply was guaranteed as long as I was willing to listen to those ideas and take action.

When the day came, it was a very harmonious, six-hour, almost painless birth at home in our bedroom. Don't get me wrong, it was a lot of work, but because we had handled the fear all along the way, the birth of our daughter was virtually pain free.

During birth classes, we were told that contractions would start slowly and then increase in frequency and intensity. By my third contraction, they came every two minutes and were i-n-t-e-n-s-e. I was a little nervous that the intensity would increase. What I didn't know was that I was already in full-on labor and my contractions were at the peak of intensity. With this realization came a release of apprehension. The direct correlation between fear and what could be identified as pain became obvious. I could lean into the work of it, and as long as

I remained fearless, there was virtually no pain — intensity and hard work, yes, but not pain.

I noticed that the only times I dealt with pain during the process was when fear crept in, fear of the unknown or fear that something was out of control. The fear and the pain were directly connected. When I was able to release the fear, the pain left. This happened specifically at two junctures, once when my water didn't break and the baby was being delivered "in the caul," and then when her head was stuck because she was coming through the birth canal "military style" so the widest part of her head was presenting instead of the point of her head. When I was able to address the fear in my thought by knowing all was working out naturally and any support needed was right with me, the fear left and so did the pain.

Two years later, our son arrived the same way, born at home. This time in about three hours and without pain.

So much of the walk of parenthood, from birth to them leaving the nest is about seeing them as whole individuals, not "mini-mes" under our control. I constantly worked on releasing them to God at every age, recognizing that they were God's children and we had the opportunity to be their parents for the time. No matter what issues came up along the way, this perspective brought healing, safety, and an assurance that they were guided and governed by a power much larger than anything we could bring as parents.

*what we hold in thought is a sovereign
responsibility, especially as parents*

Our roles as parents transition from an egoic perspective of being the
parent and being responsible for the well-being of the child to the more
divine perspective of God being the Parent, and our full response-ability
— our ability to respond to God as the divine Parent, always guarding,
guiding, protecting, governing. Then we let go of our identity as the
parent and choose instead to reflect God's parenthood purely.

One time, our daughter had a very high fever that kept getting
worse. We prayed, but I couldn't get beyond the fear and a personal
sense of responsibility. After a full day with the fever not abating,
we were both very concerned and on the verge of taking her to the
emergency room, but we held back. Spiritual healing had been an
effective approach my entire life, and we wanted the best for our
daughter. I held my daughter in my arms in a sky chair outside on
the deck. She was burning up. I was scared. We called the spiritual
practitioner we'd been working with. J. talked with him and relayed
our fears. Within thirty seconds of that phone call, I felt the fever
drain from my daughter's body and her temperature drop. The
healing was so fast, it seemed almost impossible. From that moment
on, she was her normal self, alert and talkative and asking for food.

Again, the healing came when the fear was removed. Just as my
mom had with her three children, I experienced leaning on divine
Love as the First Aid, which brought healing, fast recovery, and
protection from harm. Critics of this prayerful approach when I was
younger focused on hypotheticals and "what if" scenarios. So as a
parent, I felt an awesome responsibility to be very clear about my

choice. This way of thinking, choosing to rely on Love instead of being driven by fear, guides life in a direction of more safety, harmony, and a realization that what we hold in thought is a sovereign responsibility, especially as parents.

I am grateful I was given a choice for mental autonomy very young. And though I didn't articulate it this way back then, I learned early to Look Up, rely on God, Look In and see my true self, and Look Out to see the effect of this approach on my experience. It would have felt irresponsible not to utilize this approach with our children. As adults, they would be free to choose for themselves how they approach life. The world constantly offers one way of thinking. Having another option opens a world of possibilities. Then it's up to each of us to decide for ourselves. Choosing what power we'll serve — Love or fear, God or self — gets us to squarely face our own trust in all that is holy and sacred.

 CHAPTER 26

Love Meets Us Where We Are

Trust in the Lord with all thine heart; and lean
not unto thine own understanding. In all thy ways
acknowledge him, and he shall direct thy paths.
— Proverbs 3: 5–6

One of the hardest moments of my life was when I had to kick our son out of the house. He'd gotten violent for the umpteenth time, breaking things and threatening us, and refused to get rid of the alcohol that intensified those behaviors. A few hours later, he stood outside the glass door and begged to come in, get something to eat, and take a shower. After years of trying to help him, draining savings to pay for rehab twice, nursing him back from two motorcycle accidents, making excuses for him, forgiving him over and over for being abusive, failing to uphold standards that felt right in my heart, countless Al-Anon meetings where I'd heard that I couldn't help him until he asked for my help and that I had been enabling the behavior, I finally had the courage to say, "No."

That moment is seared into my memory. I looked into my son's eyes on the other side of the glass and refused him entry because I finally understood that helping him by letting him back in excused his behavior, did not hold him accountable for his actions, and enabled him in his addiction. There will be those of you reading this who judge me, and think, "How could you!" Believe me, I was judging myself, and I still wonder if that was the best thing I could have done.

All I know is that it was the only thing I could do at that point. I had given up so much of myself for so many years — so much of what I knew to be right — by choosing to excuse, ignore, or wrongly accommodate emotional, physical, mental mistreatment, and threats. (It's hard even now to use the most accurate word, abuse.) I needed the trauma to stop. I needed to take a breath and feel safe. Rather than continue to fight against all the pain — anger, violent words and actions, all the lying and mistrust, all the shattered hopes — I finally needed to take a stand for peace and harmony, trustworthiness and responsibility, faith and love — real love — the tough kind of love that says no to abuse and violence, manipulation and lies, being used and taken for granted.

I had to stand there and realize that what was right mattered, that my husband and I mattered, and that saying no to my son was taking a stand for what was right for all of us. Saying no created the space for him to stop acting out from a place that wasn't his true self and to step into his best self. It was his choice to step into that place or not. I took a stand for what I knew was true about the love of parent and child instead of acting out the distorted, sham, imposter relationship of addict and enabler.

You know from reading this far that I pray through everything, that I ask God to show me the way, that I struggle to know the right thing to do — not what I want, but what's right. All I can say is that in that moment, it felt like the only thing I could do, and it took an enormous amount of courage.

Without getting into all the details of the years of struggle prior to and following this moment, I do want to share a few incidents that brought me to my knees, when I reached out with all my heart to find an answer and relief from suffering.

Our Needs Are Met when We Trust Love's Guidance

He'd been out of the house for about two weeks. I didn't know where he was or if he was okay. Whether you're a parent or not, you can imagine the mental and emotional walk I was on. Sleep-deprived and swimming in self-condemnation and deep wells of doubt, I decided to go for a run. Running seemed to be the only thing that would clear my head. I paused at the front gate to Look Up. I actually looked up and asked God, with tears streaming down, "I just want to know if he's alive." I Looked In. I was willing to release him and not control his journey, but I was still a mom and wanted to know if he was okay. Parents are willing to give their own life for their child's. I yearned for guidance. Anything that would give me a sense of direction. He and his friends used to talk about hanging out on what they called *God's Couch* up in the hills. I had no idea where that was, but I thought maybe he was camping there, and I was willing to try to find it. I would do anything.

I heard a voice, "Go left and go left."

It can't be that easy, I thought, questioning my ability to listen and hear intuition, arguing with the simplicity of it.

I listened deeply, humbly. This instruction took me in the opposite direction of *God's Couch*; the hills were to the right. But I did what I've always done. I Looked Out and let my actions follow the intuition. I ran left the half block to the river, down the embankment to the fence until I couldn't go any farther, and then turned left along the path, the river to my right and the embankment to my left with the street at eye level.

I ran about two blocks, watching my footing on the path and glancing around for further signs or signals. Then something made me look up the embankment. I noticed movement in the shrubs. It was my son, camped under some bushes, right next to the road. I drove by that spot multiple times a day, but from the street side, the only thing visible was the shrubbery. When I saw him, the dam of doubt and the pressure of constant questioning broke. The tears flowed. He was alive! I knew where he was.

I brought him food and supplies, which later I realized was still enabling, but at the time, it was what I needed to do as his mom to deal with the reality of the situation, which felt so foreign to our sense of life and family. This was the first of many times I was guided by intuition to find him when he was missing. In each case, my desire to know, a willingness to ask, listen, and let go of control, led me to peace.

Love Meets Our Need in a Form We Can Accept

Again, as with most of the stories I share, reason tried to argue a different path, but intuition won. With so many confirmations of intuition guiding me to a better result, I hope I'm giving you the courage to always follow yours, no matter what external evidence and matter-based reasoning would argue.

He moved away from that spot and went missing again. The image in my mom-brain was homeless, helpless, addicted. My mind spun faster and faster, narrowing perception until I was forced to release control or implode. The only pain and suffering I felt during those years was caused by my own inability to let go of control. I had to let go of my dreams for him, the life I'd always envisioned for him and for us as a family, the holidays, the family gatherings, his eventual family and children, all the accomplishments and talents realized, his success, the feeling of responsibility and purpose as a parent, seeing him fulfill his dreams and be happy — I had to let go of it all.

After he'd been missing again for another couple of weeks, I went running at two in the morning to shake off the fear and find peace. I ran along the same road where I saw him last. I spotted a police car up ahead, but they were too far away for me to flag them down and ask if they'd seen him. Then I saw them stop in the middle of the road for no apparent reason.

"Run!" came the prompting. I sprinted to catch up, flagging them down as they started to pull away again. They stopped. As soon as I started talking through my tears, the officer on the passenger side stepped out and approached me. It was the same officer that responded years before, the first time we called the police to issue a warning and help us deal with an out of control teenager. When I saw Officer B. approach me, it was like seeing an angel. He had been a pillar of strength for me at critical junctures over the years and there he was!

"Our son is missing again. I haven't seen him in two weeks," I told him.

"I've seen him hanging out at Hazeltine Park," he said. "I'll have the other officers keep an eye out for him."

Once again, synchronous information gave me the answer I needed to calm my fears and trust just a little longer that my child was being cared for by angels tangible and spiritual. It was out of my hands. I let go a little more.

Cast Out Self and Fear So Love Can Guide

Another time, our son was in a lock-down treatment facility after being picked up for erratic behavior while under the influence. He was under observation for a few days for his own safety, and my husband, daughter, and I were in the lobby waiting to visit him. We heard an urgent alert go out over the loudspeaker. Someone had gotten out. My gut feeling was that the alarm had something to do with our son. When the nurse came out to tell us we wouldn't be able to visit, it confirmed my intuition.

"What happened?" I asked.

"He refused to move away from the door, which is why your visit was delayed. When he saw an opening, he bolted past the staff into the courtyard and escaped!"

"How is that even possible?"

What she described sounded like a movie stunt; she seemed almost awestruck at the sheer skill of it. "As soon as he saw an opening, he was gone in seconds. He scaled a fifteen-foot chain link fence topped with three feet of barbed wire angled in, sprinted across the courtyard, and then basically hopped over two eight-foot cement walls like they were nothing! Nobody has ever done *that* before!" Outside those walls was a community unfamiliar to him. We'd never been in this area of California.

"What are you going to do?" I asked her.

"There's nothing we can do."

I felt the panic rising. "What do you mean? He's in your care; you're responsible for his well-being!"

"Ma'am, we have many patients. Everyone needs our care."

I felt panicked at the thought of him being out on the street not knowing the area or where he was, and due to medication they'd given him, knowing he was probably not in a good place mentally.

"The longer we wait, the farther away he'll get." I expected an urgent response from the facility. Nothing happened and nobody leaped into action. "What do you normally do in these instances?"

They stood there stunned. "People have left by sneaking out doors or not returning from a visit, but not by scaling fences to escape!"

Their only recourse was to call the police and report him missing.

Their lack of urgency and lack of attention to his safety baffled and angered me. We decided to drive around and look for him ourselves. After about twenty minutes of driving in circles, I asked my husband to pull over. The feeling of fear and panic wasn't helping. The more I grasped for control, the worse I felt — and the louder the car got, with three of us running scenarios and divergent solutions. We didn't need to *do something*. We needed to let go. I needed to get beyond my own perspective, quiet my thinking and reasoning, listen for an answer, and feel guided.

"J. pull over. I need to get out," I said with determination.

I stood on the sidewalk. I listened. Thoughts raced. I imagined how he must feel in a strange place. I was scared I'd never see him again. Reason, projection, and prediction, combined with deep love, fear, yearning, and panic, created a sludge-like stew of thoughts and emotions. I needed mental discipline to quiet the distractions of fear and emotion and get still, to stop thinking and feeling, and tune in.

I got very still. I trusted the fact of intuition — that divine intelligence was present. God was in control and guiding us and an intuition would come. I found a level of peace and waited. Listened. I must have stood on the sidewalk for five minutes. J. and Makenna sat in the car, patiently waiting. They'd seen me in this state before and knew not to interrupt.

I opened myself to inspiration and Looked Up — affirmed that God knew where he was, and I Looked In — affirmed that I was receptive to Truth and could hear the intuitions that came to me. I asked God to guide me and listened for direction, then waited with openness, an expectant pause, a receptive mental posture to hear the answer. When reasoning strained to fill the mental space, I fought to keep it open for inspiration, some kind of direction and truth. I needed to be the open channel, ready to be filled, or more accurately, expectant that it was already filled since I was a reflection of All-intelligence. Racing around to find a solution and act on it was a denial that I was already guided and already knew the answer. Calm listening would reveal the idea needed to meet the need, and then I could Look Out and act quickly.

I got a sense, a thought, a feeling, to get back in the car.

I got in. "Go that way, quickly," I said, pointing straight ahead. As J. drove, I looked down and kept listening for what was next. We drove about three blocks to the end of the street, where it intersected a busy boulevard with a median.

Listening for the next direction, I heard, "Look up." I looked up.

"There he is!" I shouted, pointing to him on the far side of four lanes of traffic as he emerged from behind a sign. My gratitude mixed with urgency. He was moving fast.

We couldn't get to the other side fast enough to track him by car, so I hopped out and tracked him on foot. Not knowing what state he was in and whether he would respond to me, I called the police for support and let them know where he was. I trusted the urgency I felt and communicated it, but it wasn't a high priority for them. I followed him for half an hour. He crossed multi-lane avenues, down side streets, in and out of fast food places to get water and probably tried to get food. I hid behind poles and kept my distance. I prayed he wouldn't turn around each time we crossed a street and I shortened the distance between us to make it across before the light changed.

223

He wandered around, clearly without a plan or consciousness of what was going on. I relayed his ever-changing location to the police and waited for them to catch up. In the end, he walked into a church and stayed there long enough to be picked up by the police and brought back to the facility. He never knew I had tracked him or had anything to do with the police finding him.

During this time it was so easy to judge myself, question if I was doing the right thing, condemn myself for not doing more, something, anything that would convince him to come home where he'd be safe and the mental pictures of the nuclear family would be realized. My heart and half the people I talked to said one thing. The 12-step meetings I attended said the opposite. And the horror of the situation took its own course. He fell between the cracks. Not addicted enough or sick enough to be committed to a program, and not well enough to have a conversation about coming home and negotiating boundaries. We were unequipped to handle this level of dysfunction. The substance-induced violent behavior towards me and J., explosive verbal abuse of me, and his absolute refusal to have a conversation with me whenever I saw him, left us no options. For us that meant the only option was turning it over to a higher power.

My Love or God's Love?

I still think about future possibilities for him. It's hard not to. But I quickly realize they don't serve anything now. I can only survive by letting go, by releasing, by turning it all over to God and realizing that "my" son is God's son and not mine. That his path is between him and his Creator. Who was I to think I knew what would make his life clear to him so that he knew his own path? I wasn't the only one being guided by God. I was being given the opportunity to trust that the same power that had always guided me was also guiding him. As long as I was in the middle of orchestrating that relationship, I was blocking the light that was meant to reach him.

Not long after that, a mom shared a story with me about her addicted son. He had called from a payphone, begging her for help, and said, "Please don't hang up!" and the phone cut out. With no way to reach him, she panicked — until she heard what she described as God's voice, very clearly saying, "As long as he can get to you, he won't get to Me."

When the mom shared that with me, my life shifted. My primal desire to love and help took a different form. It shifted from "What can I do?" to "How much can I let go and trust God? — trust that Love finds and supports the smallest amount of good and grows it bigger. I felt the aha moment to my core. Love will meet him where he is, support every bit of good deep down inside of him, and grow it bigger so that he can see his own goodness and act on that, step by step.

All my love for him poured out to pay the price of letting go.

When I got it, when the understanding landed, it was like releasing the stopper in a sink filled with all the worry and doubt and self-condemnation, all the questions about what I needed to do to fix the situation, all the guilt and shame from feeling responsible, that I must have done something wrong, or worse, the temptation to blame my husband for not being or doing . . . something . . . I wasn't even sure what. All of it poured out — down the drain — and all that was left was my love for him and love for the power larger than both of us, governing and keeping us both safe. In order to let him go and trust him to God, the price I had to pay was all my love for him and the hope of ever feeling his love for me. The stopper in my heart came loose. All my love for him poured out to pay the price of letting go. I gave it all. It was a mother's sacrifice, her entire heart for her child's life.

What I'm realizing as I write this is that we get to be supported in that equation too. When we let go and trust others to Love, we also trust ourselves to Love. When we release control and release fear of the future for others, we do so by knowing Love is present for them. In the process, we feel Love's arms wrapped around us. We can feel all the good present right here and now, Love enfolding us and radiating out in all directions to include all, love opening our awareness to the vastness of Love's infinite embrace and a feeling of comfort, peace, and wholeness. Just as fear separates us from each other, in Love we are all connected with and to each other.

There's always more to learn about letting go. Just when we think we've done it, we're offered another opportunity to let go more, release more, give up more control. And notice in all of those, we are getting rid of something rather than gaining something. So what are we gaining — moving toward — in an effort to let go, release, give up control?

We move toward trust. We trust the law of good to be in operation and allow Love and Truth to govern rather than the small ego. We embrace the idea that we are inside the whole. Rather than us letting go of control or holding onto trust, we are held by Love, held inside the control of All, and we yield to that control. We're not giving up, we're gaining a more accurate sense of what's actually going on: God is in control and always has been. Align with what is and be free.

Arrest the Error, Free the Individual

During the next several years our son remained missing, living on the streets (at this writing, he's still missing), and I didn't know if he was okay, struggling or thriving, and honestly, my worst fear came in the form of a question: was he alive? This tested my stance. When I studied karate, they tested our stance by trying to knock us over. This felt like that. The stronger I felt, the more I was challenged to hold the stance, no matter who or what tried to knock me down.

He was in and out of jail countless times. The misdemeanors stacked up for things like trespassing, sleeping in stairwells, or warrants for missing court dates. At first, I struggled to know what to do. Should I help get him out of jail? Should we fight the charges? Eventually, news of his arrest was good news. It meant he was alive, safe, housed, clothed, and fed. And it meant we could talk. I didn't think of *him* being arrested, but the *error* — the bad stuff weighing on him being arrested — while he was being freed from the struggle of survival on the street and the imposition of all the bad influences. This shift put me in gratitude. The error was arrested; he was freed. I slept better when he was in jail. I knew where he was and that he was okay for the moment.

Keep Our Thought Clear to Hear Love's Guidance

One very long stretch during his time on the street really tested my trust that God cares for His children and that our son was on his own path of learning. He'd been missing for over a year. His last contact with us was a call from Santa Barbara. He didn't sound like himself. The call was brief and disjointed. He mentioned trouble with a shelter there and a desire to head back to LA. But that was it. We had no other information.

When a work trip required me to be in Southern California for several days, all I could think about was the opportunity to find our son, to know if he was okay. He was probably there somewhere, but I had no idea where. I hesitated to think about the possibility. *Should I open up my heart to even consider looking for him? Or am I just setting myself up for a lot of hurt and pain by thinking about finding him?* With this desire came the follow-up thoughts.

- "What will you do if you find him?"

- "Will you try to get him to change what he's doing?"

- "Will you be able to have a conversation with him?"

- "Will he recognize you?"

- "Will he want to talk with you?"

- "How will you feel if you get rejected?"

- "Would this be good for you?"

- "Could you stay released and let go and trust?"

- "Will you go into a guilt spiral?"

- "Will you feel like you have to *do* something? Save him?"

The questions swirled and taunted me. The self-flagellation, the guilt, the spiral of doubt, the darkness, the yearning for healing, the obsession to know and see the end of all the trauma for him, for me, for the family . . . all of it came rushing back. Clearly, I had work to do to let go and trust God. A sense of personal responsibility still rose up inside of me. Any thought of contacting him brought it up and took center stage in my heart and mind. I had enough years of that kind of extreme thinking to know I couldn't survive more of it. I needed to keep my own mental boundaries clear.

Then I put both hands on my heart and said,
"I am loved. I am safe. God is here. All is well.

I steadied my own mental and emotional stance by sticking to what I knew to be absolutely true. I practiced Up-In-Out. God knows who he is. God sees him and knows where he is. He is cared for and given the ideas he needs to stay safe and healthy. I checked my own thoughts and beliefs to see if they lined up with the absolute. I affirmed that I knew that was true and tuned in to any intuitive thought that would bring comfort.

I kept myself from imagining horror stories, which were too easy to get hooked by, feel strung up by, and then be left to hang and emotionally bleed out. Was he on drugs, suffering without housing, hungry and begging for food or money, stealing to survive, getting mixed up with addicts and horrible role models, going down a slippery slope that leads to sickness and death? The darkest, worst-case, scariest scenarios presented themselves in vivid color. It took all my strength to counter them.

I played a game with myself.

"Do you know where he is?"

"No."

"Do you know if he's okay?"

"No, but I must claim that he is, or I'll break into a million pieces."

"Am I okay right now?"

"Yes."

"Is he cared for right now?"

"Yes, by God."

"Can I trust God?"

"Yes."

"What's the best thing I can do for him right now?"

"Love him and turn him over to God. That's the best I can do."

Then I put both hands on my heart and said, "I am loved. I am safe. God is here. All is well." I repeated this over and over until my insides calmed down and I actually believed and trusted the words. Then I said, "He is loved. He is safe. God is with him wherever he goes. All is well."

I continued until I was able to let go of everything except my desire to know if he was alive. That's all I asked for, "Just let me know if he's alive." The rest of his story and his path I trusted to God.

I had three days of intense work meetings in San Diego with no bandwidth to look for him. I continued to keep myself calm by affirming good. My husband had come with me on the trip, and the next day we were to drive north to catch a plane out of Burbank back home to Washington. We left room in the schedule to see how we felt in the moment about looking for our son.

Trust God With Our Desire

I woke up very early that last morning to pray. I Looked Up with all my heart. "I know You know where he is. What would You have me know?" I just wanted to know if he was alive. I Looked In and affirmed that I was a reflection of the all-knowing Mind, and since Mind knew where he was, I could too. I needed to be in a state of peace and stay out of personal attachment or emotion if I wanted to be clear enough to hear any divine intuition or guidance. I affirmed God's government and guidance of all. I affirmed my trust of the divine laws holding everything and everyone in balance and order.

My desire was to be at peace and completely tuned in, to know my true self wholly and completely so that no emotional triggers would distract me. I needed to be completely released from any desired outcome. If it was right for me to know where he was, I would. Every personal outcome I could imagine had to be discarded and barred from entering consciousness. It took effort. I had to trust and release and keep at it.

Truth is always precise and aligned. It is a misperception of truth that is off and looks like a mess or lack of precision. The precision of Truth is the reality. With my sense of Truth clear of distraction or false pictures, I could Look Out and expect to see my experience align with harmony, peace, fulfillment, abundance, and all that is included in Love.

We drove north on the 405, my mental posture expectant and open, trusting and humble, yielding to divine Love's control. J. and I hadn't yet decided if we would look for our son before we flew out. I was open to being guided and hearing some direction, but I didn't know if I would hear anything.

Just before the airport, I started getting a strong feeling that we should get off the freeway and drive surface streets along the coast. I asked J. to get off at the next exit. We continued north and wove our way toward the beach. As we entered Venice, I said, "I need to walk the boardwalk."

J. found a place to pull over three blocks later. It was mid-day on a warm, sunny Saturday in November, the day before our son's birthday. I grabbed a bottle of water, my baseball cap, and my phone with his picture pulled up. I walked back the three blocks to where I had heard the instruction and turned toward the boardwalk. J. continued driving north to park at the Santa Monica end of the beach to walk south, while I started at the south end in Venice and planned to walk north.

I listened. I knew the same voice would keep guiding me. The boardwalk was jammed with people and activity. Crowds gathered around performers, while skateboarders, roller bladers, and joggers whizzed past in both directions. Music and the smell of fried food filled the air. I listened — tuned in to intuition and internal stillness — and stayed open to more direction. As soon as I reached the boardwalk, I saw one particular homeless guy who stood out to me. I approached him, and shielding my phone from the glare, showed him the picture of my son.

"I know that guy," he said. "Nice guy. I haven't seen him around for a while, but nice guy."

I walked about ten steps heading north and another person stood out. It was another homeless guy. I showed him, again, shielding my phone from the sun so he could make out the image.

"Ya, I know him," he said. "I saw him this morning up at that restroom!" pointing to the concrete block of public restrooms ahead.

My insides were buzzing. I had confirmation that he was alive and had been seen that morning right in that area! Could I trust it? Were these guys telling the truth? Did they really know him, or were they just trying to connect with me to get something they needed or hoped I would pay them? None of those feelings were present when I interacted with them, but my mind started racing.

Before I walked toward the restroom, I took a moment to calm myself and clear my thought of anything negative, any personal agenda, or expected outcome. I regained my peace — got back into trusting the flow of what was happening. The process I use to do this is a mini version of Look Up, Look In, Look Out. Acknowledge one Mind. Claim that I am the manifestation of that Mind, and know that I will see evidence of that Mind in my experience. Calm all fear by knowing that I am loved, I am safe, God is here, all is well. Declare the basis of God and my being. Affirm that all are governed by the same Love from which we can never be separated. And materially based suggestions can never overrule the power of Love.

I walked north. Right near the restroom there was another homeless guy moving his sleeping bag toward the retaining wall on the edge of the boardwalk. I asked him how long he'd been on the street and if he was in touch with his parents. He said no, not for a long time. As we chatted, an official-looking guy with security badges hanging around his neck and wearing a vest that said "Joseph" approached us and offered the homeless guy a bottle of water.

Joseph was there to help the homeless and had just started working the beach beat that day. I thought maybe meeting Joseph was why I was guided to this spot. I showed Joseph my son's picture and gave him my details. I asked if he could keep an eye out for Kelemn and text me if he saw him — if he could be my eyes and ears on the beach since I lived out of state and was flying out in a few hours. He agreed.

I felt complete, like I'd received an answer. I had confirmation that he'd been seen that day and was alive. I established a link to the area with someone who had his best interest in mind. But then I heard a very clear direction, "Start walking north, now!"

I quickly thanked Joseph and started walking. I was looking down to stay focused and not get distracted by all the people, sights, and sounds. Then another instruction, "Look up!" I looked up. Walking very quickly in my direction was a disheveled guy with really long bleached red hair and a beard. I recognized his gait right away. It was him! As we got closer to each other, I didn't know what to say. He looked right through me as he approached. I wasn't sure if he recognized me or not.

"Hi Kelemn!"

"Get the fuck away from me!" he shouted as he brushed passed just a few feet away.

"It's your birthday tomorrow."

He stopped, spun back toward me, held out his hand, and glared at me, "Give me money, then!"

I hadn't prepared for a conversation. "I'm sorry, I don't have any cash," I blurted.

"Get the fuck away from me, then. Leave me alone!" He walked away quickly.

I panicked a bit. I thought about how different he looked. Thought about taking a picture of him and filing a missing person report later that day. Thought about the past and the future all at once — that happy, caring, intelligent, and curious boy — and wondered if I would remember that version of him in the future. Would I remember what he looked like before or even what he looked like now? What if I never saw him again?

Hold On and Let Go

I wanted to hold on and had to let go. There was nothing I could do to change anything about the circumstance. I knew that if he didn't want help, nothing I could do would be helpful; it would be enabling. The path he was on veered away from me. I paused to leave some space and then followed behind so I wasn't in his line of sight. I fumbled with my phone to secretly take a picture so he wouldn't get angry. I took several by holding the phone down by my side, hoping that I was capturing something.

He saw what I was doing and stopped and turned in a rage. "Get the fuck away from me and stop following me!"

People stopped and turned toward me, the object of his anger, and asked me if everything was okay. "Yes, he's my son," I said. They went back to their day.

I had to respect his request. I watched him walk away and sit on a wall by one of the restrooms. He faced the ocean with his back to me. I kept walking but at a distance. He didn't turn around, clearly disinterested in whether I was there or not. It was over. That was the only interaction I would have for the time being. I let go of any other possibility of connection or communication. I was grateful to have found him and gotten an answer to my prayer. He was alive and seemed to be okay physically.

you, too, can trust the voice within

I took a picture of the name of the cross street so I could remember where he was last seen in case I wanted to file a missing person report with the police once I returned home.

The main reason I shared this with you was to give you an example of the sheer precision of what's available to us when we ask and tune in. Humanly, the odds of finding someone in the state of California when you have no idea where they are or if they are even alive are astronomical. But there you have it. Not astronomical to God. Easy, clear, precise, surgical even. Beyond a needle in a haystack. Once again, I'd been given what I needed to go on another day, another month, another year. I trusted that I would be guided when I needed an answer.

I assure you that you, too, can trust the voice within. You, too, can know that answers are available to you when you ask and look beyond the external evidence. You, too, have the ability to listen, follow, and be guided to find the answers to the questions in your heart. Know that you have the simple tool, Look Up, Look In, Look Out. Know that God, the governing force of the universe, is also governing all of us and keeping everything aligned as it should be to maintain balance and abundance.

EXERCISE

Take stock of your thinking. How are you viewing the outward physical picture?

Are you viewing the physical as governed by matter? The physical, when seen through a material lens with thought governed by material law, will confirm all the limitations of matter.

Are you viewing the physical as governed by the Divine? The physical, when seen through a spiritual lens with thought governed by divine law, will confirm the limitless reality of Spirit — truth revealed by spiritual intuition and known and felt by our heart and true self.

Practice managing thought and emotion so that you know your ability to do this when needed.

Whenever you feel fear and doubt, and are stuck and overwhelmed by circumstance, take hold of your thought and govern it. Proactively shift your focus from out there to within. Put your hands on your heart and dwell on these ideas until you feel a sense of calm and recognize these words as the truth.

I am loved.
I am safe.
God is here.
All is well.
And I know it.
And I feel it.

PART 6

Let Go and Let God

We all must let go of the externals as our measure of identity and worth. We are not measured by our age, our children, bank account, height or weight, our address, position or title, awards or accolades, wardrobe, our social media following, or number of admirers.

When we let go of all of that, do we see who we are? Who are we without all the numbers? Let it all go. Now who do you see?

We must let go of ourselves to be fully ourselves as the expression of the divine. Let go of *me* to be the fullest expression of *Me*. Let God be All. Sounds a little silly to think that we have anything to say about that, since God is All, but as long as we hold onto a little me and a smaller vision of life, that's what we'll experience. Life is poised to express itself fully as us — just waiting for us to let go of our concept, our will, our plans, our loves, fears, dreams — our everything. When we give our whole heart to God, God leads us to our whole heart. Our purpose becomes obvious. We walk on the path of serving others. Our whole being is the expression of good, and the effect of good is seen in healing all around us.

Do we focus on *letting go* of something or *holding on*to something? We can more easily let go of control when we know — and hold onto — God's control. Imagine what our world would be like if we all let go and let God.

CHAPTER 27

Let Go of Control

Step by step will those who trust Him find that
"God is our refuge and strength, a very present help in trouble."
— Mary Baker Eddy

A parent is on the journey of letting go of control throughout their child's whole life. Parents learn early that controlling children is not an effective strategy. Controlling their every move and choice deprives them of opportunities to make decisions, know themselves, and master self-control. When addiction is introduced into the mix, the desire for control and need to release control escalates. With our son, I had two choices, control more, feel more pain, and become more enabling, or release more, feel less pain, and speed the path to healing. I practiced letting go on deeper and deeper levels.

When Kelemn was offered a treatment program instead of jail for the third time, I felt deep relief. When he walked away as soon as he arrived at the program, I was tempted to feel sad and anxious because it meant he was back on the street. Supported by my spiritual practice, I moved quickly to release. Sadness came up, of course, but the place of release came from the knowledge that his journey is between him and God and not my business. My business is to love him and let him go. I don't know what will bring him closer to his true self. Maybe this is the exact path he needs for his own growth. If I insert myself into his journey by trying to manipulate or change it, I'm saying my way is better than Love's way; I'm saying I don't trust that God has him or trust that he can hear God's guidance. In those moments, I ask myself, *Do I deeply trust that Love is governing?*

LOOK UP LOOK IN LOOK OUT

How do I walk away from control and anxiety and move towards trust? Look Up, Look In, Look Out. Affirm God's power and presence, affirm Kelemn's individual inherent connection to Source separate from me, and affirm that his expression of life must align with Life and Truth, not me.

Once I find the place of calm knowing, I sit on my hands and stay out of the way. I trust that he is being guided by his own internal spiritual GPS and that he hears that guidance loud and clear. I continually, and I do mean continually, trust that he is being guided — that divine Mind is his mind, that he reflects all the light of Mind, and that he can never be separated from the source of his reflection. If I'm ever tempted to take an action, make a call, reach out, drive around looking for him, offer guidance, I only take that action if it is prompted by inspiration and divine intuition. I reject any action prompted by fear, concern, or any assumption that my opinion of his life and what it "should" look like is the "right" way. As long as my actions are impelled by Love, divine Love, I know I'm operating within the law of good, and therefore only good could ever come of that.

So each time I'm tempted to act in response to circumstance, I pause, Look Up, Look In, and Look Out. Am I knowing and claiming the allness of Good? Am I seeing myself as the reflection of all good? Am I seeing him as the son of God? If all of those are in place, then I listen for divine guidance and take the divinely impelled action. I do that over and over again, sometimes better than other times. Honestly, when I charge ahead thinking I know the answer and need to do something right away, I feel sad, stressed, out of control, panicked, and full of fear for him and for me. The only freedom I can find is when I let go of control and turn it all over to a higher power.

Those who have gone through 12-step programs or worked through and overcome codependency or addiction know this walk intimately. Surrender is the only solution for us and for them. But knowing that we are surrendering to an all-powerful Love brings comfort, release, and the knowledge that the best possible care is available to them when we get out of the way and don't block the light. Remember, "As long as he can get to you, he won't get to Me." That is powerful.

Twice now, when I've been pulled by the pain of not knowing where he is, how he's doing, or if he's alive, I've had a profound experience of having my heart touched deeply in a moment of Truth. The first time was when I was reading a story in the Bible about the prophet Elijah helping a widow whose child had died. In the story Elijah says, "Give me your son." And it says he took the child from her, laid the child on his bed, and ultimately brought the child back alive. That morning, though I'd read that story countless times before and knew it well, I read not that Elijah took the child, but that the mom *gave her child to Elijah.* As a mom, I felt deep empathy for her. I burst into tears, totally releasing my own son to God. I cried a deep heaving release, and in seconds, it was over. I had let go of the last vestige of control.

Letting go of outlining results
opens the space for possibilities.

He called that night. I hadn't heard from him in almost a year and a half. He'd been missing on the street. When I released my hold on him and any expectation that our connection should look a certain way, there was space for him to reach out. I don't think that's a coincidence.

The other time this deep release happened was when I saw a video of an artist. She was painting a large canvas, about three feet by four feet. The video itself is poetic — a sped up view of the painting coming to life. At the end, the full image is revealed — Jesus holding a lamb. The caption reads, "He left the 99 to go after 'The One Who Lost Its Way.'"

It happened again. I burst into tears, briefly, but from an ocean-trench depth of grief. Moments later, I received an email with the information I needed to find out where he was, and I knew he was okay.

Letting go of outlining results opens the space for possibilities. Because I released a personal grip on what things should look like and let go of my fear of negative results by trusting the power larger than me, I made space for a new answer. I was open for good to flow in from the higher power, fill the space, and appear to me in the moment.

Letting go of human reasoning has been possible for me in proportion to my willingness to lean on God and trust the infinite allness of Spirit, trust the all-knowing Mind, and trust that the divine law governing all reality is operating. This truth can be seen clearly when looking through the spiritual lens but will seem warped when looking through the material, limited, fear-based lens.

We always have the choice to Look Up, Look In, and Look Out and see with our spiritual senses. We grow into our practice. It is the tough moments of letting go that test us. We get better each time we turn a tough moment into an opportunity to let go, each time we use the tools we have to move from fear and anxiety into trust and release, and each time we look beyond limits and finite appearance to see the infinitude of good available to all of us. We have the choice. The choice matters because the choice we make in those moments determines whether our experience pushes us down or lifts us up.

CHAPTER 28

Yield to Divine Purpose

One can never go up, until one has gone down in his own esteem.
— Mary Baker Eddy

I was on my knees on the floor of my office, again turning my life over to God. I was searching for guidance on whether The Institute for Spiritual Fitness (ISF), which I'd founded a few years before, was the right direction for my life. In usual fashion, I reached out, asking God to show me what was the next right step.

My voice teacher (I'd been a soloist for years at a local church), had just challenged me to "get out there" into the world again. I'd spent the last five years caring for two small children and cobbling together work in the form of several different jobs: phone survey researcher, a tutoring business, freelance reporter for the wire services, book editor, emerging voice-over artist and actress, and as I'd done since college, spiritual practitioner, praying for people who asked for metaphysical support. My heart still pulled in the direction of my calling — to serve God, live by the laws of God, and demonstrate the healing power of God the way Jesus did.

I have felt pulled by this love of God my whole life and yearned to understand the Truth behind Jesus' healings. He knew he was the Son of God and the embodiment of Christ. He revealed this Truth. He proved the power of Love in healing and resurrection, that Love is always present to heal every aspect of this experience, and that this Truth is a divine Science to be demonstrated, as I've seen demonstrated throughout my life.

That's why The Institute for Spiritual Fitness came about. I wanted to create a space in which everyone could see the connection between our spiritual fitness and its effect on our lives, our work, our businesses, and the world. I felt guided to set it up and didn't have a clue about starting a real business or nonprofit.

As I knelt on the floor, listening for direction, the phone rang. It was Berkeley Hall's head of school, where I regularly worked as a substitute teacher and at one point, jumped in as the full-time drama teacher for a semester.

"Our receptionist just walked out the front door and said she wasn't coming back. Could you start full-time tomorrow?"

I knew the job; I had subbed many times. The role required a very particular set of skills and a knowledge of their systems and school culture, protocols, etc. I knew I could do it, but my ego was none-too-pleased when I heard what he was asking of me. I had been a TV news anchor and producer, had a blossoming career as an actress, and was starting the spiritual company I'd been intuitively guided to start. I thought I had bigger fish to fry. Why was I being offered an entry level administrative role?

The timing of the call, moments after I'd turned my future over to God — again — was what made me pay close attention.

I asked God to show me next steps, but was this my answer? Was I being asked to start at the bottom again, let go of ego, and be humble enough to serve? Was this really what God wanted of me? The questions galloped through, kicking up the dust of false ego and clouding the way forward. I needed quiet and stillness to hear the answer.

"Let me pray about it," I said in all sincerity. "Can I let you know in a few hours?" He was also a praying man and understood this choice deserved the attention of heart and not just head.

It made no sense in terms of a career. It made no sense in terms of following the path of the ISF. It made a little bit of sense financially and logistically since both our children attended Berkeley Hall and employees received a break on tuition. The list of pros and cons started to scroll in my head. And then I stopped the scroll. I became peaceful and listened. I pushed out all the temptations to calculate or reason through where this would lead or how it would look. In that place of peace and stillness, it felt right, calm, and directed. It wasn't what I would have chosen on any level if you'd laid out options in front of me, but it was what was being asked of me.

Little did I know that working at Berkeley Hall School (BHS) would be the place of my refining — blade on blade — the place where ego's edges softened and truth's precision sharpened. And control was unhooked. I had many jobs over the almost twenty years at BHS, each of them demanding and honing skills that came naturally. At each transition, just like when I worked at The Monitor Channel, I trusted God to guide me to where I could serve most, and I was never steered wrong.

This period earned me a master's degree in letting go. I let go of more than I ever thought possible. Everywhere in my life, family, friends, work, church, I let go of control, let go of outlining outcomes, let go of my will, my opinion, my sense of right and wrong, let go of judgment, and my way of doing things.

At the ten-year mark working at BHS, I felt the pull to move on to something new. But when I turned to the Up-In-Out way of discerning the right path, I found that I needed to go deeper into the organization and play a bigger role. I supported a new head of school, trained teachers, parents, and students in a new system I'd set up, and made a mandatory move from a corner office to a bullpen-style open floor plan, which all demanded more humility and more letting go of control.

"It's not about me!" became the silent warrior cry of my heart. I mentally shaved back the need to be seen, the need to be appreciated, the need to find worthiness in externals, and every other form of ego accommodation. One of the big tests was letting go of reputation and image. A campaign of lies waged to discredit me and the work I'd done for years came to a head. Rather than racing in to defend myself, I decided to let my work speak for itself. When the renegade teacher's efforts were discovered, my character stood the test. I had walked through the gauntlet with grace and humility without defending or attacking, without chest-pumping or whining. I kept my mouth shut, put my head down, and realized there was nothing I could do to control what others thought of me. And more than that, I didn't *want* to control what others thought of me because it was none of my business, and it would be a waste of time.

I needed to change my thinking if I wanted
to see a change in my experience.

When we finally stop trying to run the world and everyone in it, even on subtle levels, it's a whole lot less stressful, and it leaves a whole lot more time to do the real work of seeing others with compassion and love. Many times that requires us to let go. Let go of control, judgment, justification, expectation, and sometimes our sense of what justice should look like. The rights and wrongs, shoulds and musts get softened into grace and compassion.

Whenever I felt unseen, unheard, unappreciated, or disrespected at work, it was because I was immersed in the fog of my own ego, thinking I had the answer and nobody would hear me. It was physically exhausting to carry the burden of knowing "the answer" and carry the anger aimed at those who didn't see it the "right" way. In those moments, I realized nothing would change until I changed. My experience was based on my thoughts. I needed to change my thinking if I wanted to see a change in my experience.

I actively let go of judgment, outlining, or imagining that there was only one solution (mine) to the issues being faced. I actively pursued seeing the bigger picture and all the forces at play. What would it be like to be in their shoes with their responsibilities and all the people gunning for them? Who did they need to answer to and what was demanded of them? As one who easily saw the big picture as well as the minutiae, this wasn't a stretch for me, but many times I still ended up in a place of anger. Logic and evidence didn't help. All the externals, no matter which direction I looked, no matter how much reason and big-picture thinking I applied, did not erase feeling unseen, unheard, and undervalued.

When the struggle finally felt too big, I turned to what I knew would work. Look Up, Look In, Look Out. Out of pain and frustration, I was forced to pray. It was a last resort for my ego, which was holding on for dear life to a smaller and smaller life ring of justification.

Working through the issue always followed the same pattern — you know it well by now. I Looked Up — reasoned who God is (in control, source of all good, true employer, all-action, all-compassion, all-understanding), and then I Looked In — reasoned who I am (reflecting all of God, fully employed to do good, compassionate, understanding, governed, guided, cared for), and then I Looked Out — reasoned who others are. (They are governed by the same law of love and adjustment and reflect the same ability to hear the truth as I do.) Only by looking out with compassion for all the players was I able to let go of outcome, anger, and judgment. Only by trusting that God is in control was I able to relax and let go of my own willful, self-justified perspective.

When I am able to detach my ego and my value from the problem or situation and see it impersonally, I am able to let the solution reveal itself naturally.

This description of finally letting go of ego's hold may remind you of a circumstance you've been in or perhaps currently find yourself in. Know that you can turn inward to resolve the issue. Know that you have the mental discipline to corral all the negative thoughts and emotions. This is not to blindly deny that you are thinking or feeling negatively towards others, but that these thoughts and feelings are not who you are! You can see them come up. Think about them. Feel them. Let them go by. And then choose to love. But how?

It helps me to realize that as long as I sit in the problem, I am not open to the answer. In order to have a hand open to receive an answer, I must first let go of the problem. Once I recognize that, I'm more willing to reach for the answer and let go of the problem. Dwelling on the possibility of love and forgiveness even in the midst of anger and hate is a foot in the door. Once that foot is planted firmly in the door, there's hope of forgiveness, perspective, or a solution. Thought has shifted. This shift is the beginning of healing, the beginning of seeing the reality that love is present right where you were blind to it moments before.

If we are open to the possibility of resolution, we look for evidence of resolution instead of stacking up more evidence of a solid, unsolvable problem. Then the whole leg is through the door. I start looking for more possibilities of resolution and more evidence. I'm open to hearing the other side's perspective. I open my ears, mind, and heart. I feel compassion that they are doing their best after all. I catch a glimmer of what this scenario looks like from where they sit. I see that they have different needs and wants, needs and wants that perhaps I am able to fulfill but did not see before. This all boils down to letting go of self. Letting go of my way as the right way, and my perspective as the only perspective. And to top it off, letting go of my worth and value being based on whether my solution is the one chosen and acknowledged as "right."

This may sound basic to anyone who has worked in teams in a professional environment. "Of course!" you're saying to yourself. "Everyone knows that!" But if we can consciously recognize what's going on in these moments, we can short-circuit the process the next time, and leapfrog over the delay prompted by our ego.

A very personal sense of ourselves holds us separate from others. Letting go of that opens our eyes to our collective oneness and union of hearts. It opens us to the heart-song sung by us all. Our lives, if we listen closely and follow, find a way to express our true self. The path is not often linear, and it may not outwardly appear the way it feels inwardly (yet), but with patience and persistence, our outward life becomes the demonstration of our inner knowing, albeit faltering and incomplete. Our prayer is that the mirror is clean and the reflection is true, that the choices we make will be true to the inner knowing just a little more each moment, each hour, each day, for as long as we have to do it.

CHAPTER 29

Make Space for Your Calling

Thou to whose power our hope we give,
Free us from human strife.
Fed by Thy love divine we live,
For Love alone is Life;
And life most sweet, as heart to heart
Speaks kindly when we meet and part.
— Mary Baker Eddy

My time at Berkeley Hall was drawing to a close. I felt it. But I couldn't see how it would happen. It had been forty years since my "near Life experience" when I faced a choice to stay on the planet or not, had the revelation that Love is all there is, and knew I was called to share the Truth I'd been shown. I decided to stay on the planet for a reason, and I hadn't fulfilled that yet. And the biblical parallel of the Israelites wandering in the wilderness for forty years was not lost on me.

I felt an urgency to fulfill my calling. I knew there was more for me to do. And the work at the school no longer drew me in the way it used to. Would I ever devote my whole life to healing and sharing Truth? Would I come to the end and meet the person I could have been, the person who made one different choice? Would I wonder, "Why didn't I? What stopped me?" Or would I trust this call to more spiritual pursuits and know I didn't need to figure out what it looked like ahead of time?

I wrestled to find clarity. I wrote lists of pros and cons. I focused on what I would gain, instead of what I would lose. I released it to God and listened. I Looked Up — I affirmed God is my life and God is in control.

I Looked In — I affirmed I am the reflection of all good, my life is purposeful by nature, and it is right for me to feel fulfilled by who I am called to be and what I'm led to do. And I Looked Out — I released the outcome. I truly wanted whatever God wanted. I was willing to give my all and serve, even without knowing the next step. Life knew I still had more letting go to do, and the lessons came in an avalanche.

Catastrophe hit at home. In just six months, my dad died; our son totaled my car; the cat died; the dog died; our son drove his motorcycle off a cliff and miraculously hit the one tree that kept him from plummeting two hundred feet; my sister-in-law died; Mom had a heart attack and underwent surgery; and then our son, riding his motorcycle, T-boned an SUV that illegally turned in front of him. He was catapulted over the vehicle and slammed onto the pavement. Gratefully, he walked away with minor injuries. But once again, the fear of loss hit hard.

I had a choice: focus on Life or loss, Love or fear. After so much letting go, I wondered — what else would I have to release, and in what form would it come?

Out of necessity, constant prayer became my waking way of being. Sleep deprivation and the relentless pounding emotional waves of death, loss, and chaos became scarily normal. The power of Love and Life supported my mom's healing as well as mine. In three months, Mom moved back to her apartment in an independent-living community in Laguna Hills — an hour or three away, depending on traffic.

I commuted every day to support her. I arrived at work two hours early, left before rush hour to get to Laguna, kept working once I arrived, then fixed Mom dinner and spent the evening visiting, cleaning, shopping, or prepping food until she went to bed. I drove home around midnight when traffic was light, and the next day, I did it all again.

After six months of this schedule, Mummy began needing even more care, and tensions at home with Kelemn were rising.

Then one night, the phone rang at 2:00 a.m., jolting me awake.

"Mom, can you come to the hospital? I was in an accident."

A nurse explained that at the scene of the motorcycle crash, he'd been bleeding out on the street and was rushed to the UCLA trauma unit with a torn artery and a shattered wrist.

Now I was caring for both Mom and Kelemn, and the schedule became even more intense. Recognizing the toll it was taking on me, and needing more care than I could manage, Mom decided to go to a nursing facility for a few days to give everyone a break.

The facility was close to where we lived, which made my commute easier. I stayed late and arrived early. While she was there, she was moved to three different rooms as her need for care increased from one day to the next. Within five days of checking into the facility, she passed on quietly and peacefully. It was completely unexpected — she had only gone there to rest for a few days. Her words as she left her apartment the week before rang in my ears.

"So this is it? I won't be coming back?"

At the time, I assured her, "Of course you'll be back. This is just for you to get your feet under you and have more support during the times I can't be here."

Little did I know she knew something that I didn't.

Her passing prompted me to let go with love, and I felt completely released from grief. When feelings of sadness tried to creep in, I reminded myself how much love I felt. And that filled me with love for "my Mummy." There was no room for sadness or grief.

The night she passed, I walked out to my car, got in, started to back out almost on auto-pilot. Then I stopped, pulled back in, and turned off the car. I got out and stood on the grassy front lawn nestled in the pines. I looked up through the branches in the stillness of night, a circle of treetops framing my gaze. The black sky and bright stars filled my awareness. The immensity of space.

"I love you, Mummy!" I whispered as my tears fell softly. I felt full of love and release rather than emptiness. A spaciousness opened in me, the place that had been occupied by the last remaining sense of responsibility I had held for my mom. She was free and so was I.

I got back in the car to head home, and hit *source* and *Bluetooth* on the dashboard — the same way I'd done every time I started the car since I'd bought it four years before — and as I drove out of the facility, the CD player started to play by itself. I hadn't touched it or played a CD for years — I didn't even know one was in there. I heard a voice reading a passage from a book my mom had introduced to me when I was a child. It was the perfect passage that might as well have been given to me directly from Mummy. It was about the ever presence of eternal Life and infinite Love. I knew she was there. I felt her. I smiled through the tears and felt joy and the fullness of our love, grateful for our mother-daughter relationship and deep friendship.

I cleaned out her apartment and let go of more family treasures than I thought possible. The Limoges, the linen, the crystal, family heirlooms from Swiss generations past, it all got hauled away. Letting go of things became the practice, but not because it felt comfortable or came from a place of release, but because I was pressed by circumstance and exhaustion. Eventually we accept where things are and the fact that it will all get thrown away at some point, so it might as well be now. It became one more opportunity to practice letting go — of overwhelm, of control, of outlining, of my world as I knew it. With both parents gone now, I had no excuse but to see myself in terms of who I was truly meant to be and what I was called to do.

✲ CHAPTER 30 ✲

Follow Your Calling The Up-In-Out Way

All things work together for good to them who love God,
to them who are called according to his purpose.
— Romans 8:28

The importance of living Look Up, Look In, Look Out in a constant way rather than applying it as a process to particular parts of my life or situations became more and more obvious. All aspects of my life came under the scrutiny of this lens. In every situation, I'd ask myself, *Does this reflect who I am? When I Look Out, does it match what I see when I Look In and when I Look Up.*

The yearning to break free from the nine-to-five and live a spiritually focused life mirrored the yearning to simplify my life in other ways. I wanted to break free from all aspects of work, relationships, and living circumstances that didn't align fully with who I was. Having everything line up with who I was at my core felt increasingly necessary.

After Mom's passing, I transitioned to full-time remote work, well before COVID hit, and so I was well prepared to handle the lockdown and remoteness imposed on us all when it came. Our subsequent move out of state solidified my remote employment status.

I had let go of my ties to family, my ties to geography, and I learned to let go of my ties to an employer. When we let go of the outcome crafted by ego, we leave space open to see what is provided by divine Ego.

It didn't matter what I did for work; it only mattered that I was truly myself while I did it. We delude ourselves into thinking that having a job is secure, when in fact, the only thing that is secure is who we are and the choice we make to express that fully or not, whether we are employed by someone else or ourselves. As with the house, being me was not contingent on the form of my job, but I wasn't expressing all of myself yet. I was still compromising the yearning within me. If I wanted to see the full expression of myself in home or work, I had to be willing to think about it differently. I had to stop compromising my heart's desire, let go of the form, and hold to the truth that I could express every aspect of myself in full alignment. I could be fully utilized in work that was completely spiritually focused.

It was clear that the desire to be who I felt called to be wasn't subsiding. I knew I needed to face it or give it up. I also knew that giving it up was not an option. So there it was! My only option was to follow the pull, the ultimate intuition to align with my highest self. I didn't want to get to the end and wonder, *What if I'd left the job? What if I'd followed my calling and shown up fully as me?*

In order to fulfill my calling, I needed to get over myself. Saying "my calling" is a bit misleading, since it wasn't about me. I was on a journey of letting go of all my wants. At the end of each path of my want or my will, I arrived at a choice: hold on or let go. Every time I held on, the cycle would continue, and I would face the same choice again. Each time I let go, I advanced to another opportunity to let go and see more of the All. Each time I let go of seeing myself in terms of my wants and will, the more I saw of Life itself and therefore more of my true self. I realized over and over that it wasn't about getting what I wanted, unless what I wanted was what Life wanted. It wasn't about serving self, but serving Life. It's this odd juxtaposition of letting go of self and at the same time fulfilling true self. I needed to embrace this idea in order to take the next steps.

Letting go of self became preservation of self.

As long as I was identified as a self, separate from Life or Source, I was stuck trying to fulfill a limited mission and view of my path. When I identified wholly with being the instrument of the divine, I was able to envision letting go of the *job* because it was no longer about what I was doing, it was about who I was being. This allowed me to envision stepping into being me as the fulfillment of Life's creation, and serve the larger purpose of Life by fully being Life's individual expression.

The first Monday in August, a month after we moved to the island, I was up early for my typical routine. I took quiet time, turned thought to serving God before my feet touched the floor, went for my morning run out in nature, and settled down to stretch out on the floor while reading my Bible lesson and other inspiring writing. This has been my daily practice for over fifty years, and for over five years, it has been the way I prepare for my daily live show to members, *Morning Metaphys*, where we explore the scientific system of divine healing and what it looks like to live by divine law.

Overtaken by an urgent need to know what work would look like moving forward and feeling exhausted by wrestling with uncertainty, I Looked Up — reached out wholeheartedly to God for an answer. I was at my wits' end. Drained from struggling to know the next steps and figure it all out, I finally let it all go. All of it.

"I will do whatever you want, God. What do you want? Should I quit my job?" which translated to, "Should I be a spiritual practitioner full-time?"

I heard a very loud voice. "You work for me!" It was a very stern, loud, male voice, with a hint of a New York accent. Didn't sound like anyone I knew, but it was emphatic and pronounced. The tone was a bit like Al Pacino in *The Godfather*. That's the closest I can come to describing what I heard — powerful, insistent, definitive, and with unquestionable authority.

My response took a sassy tone: "Well, alrighty then. You figure it out!" I threw my hands in the air and put the whole mess in God's lap. I felt complete relief. I didn't have to worry about it anymore! God said I worked for Him. Okay. He's my boss. He'll tell me when, where, and how, and what it looks like. I wasn't off the hook. I was completely on God's hook, and rather than feeling constrained, I felt wholly liberated.

Within twenty-four hours, during a daily Zoom check-in, my boss told me that the position I currently held as director of communications was being phased out, replaced by two lower on-campus positions. My position would end on the last day of the month, about three weeks later. I was welcome to apply for another position, but I would have to move back to LA.

I almost laughed. I sat there thinking, *Oh, this is good! God has such a comedic sense of timing. Seriously? This was perfect!* The answer was obvious. I felt complete relief and joy. I had struggled to see my way free of this job for two years, and as soon as I turned it over to God, I got a clear answer within the day? Wow! I founded This Choice Matters the next day.

The path was made ultimately clear for me. I worked for God. J. and I now lived on an island surrounded by water with a house to remodel and make completely our own, a project we loved to do together as we had several times during our marriage. All that was left was for me to follow my calling, speak the Truth, be a living beam of Love, a lighthouse shining in the darkness to lead the way for others to find their own divine light. That's my prayer every day, to do God's work and serve Him in whatever way He leads me. To listen and follow.

Choosing to be me means being at one with God. It means being humble enough to realize that my life is God's, not a separate thing I claim to create and manage. It means being at peace as Soul's expression, whoever that leads me to be, whatever that leads me to know, whatever that leads me to see, whatever that leads me to do, wherever that leads me to go, and whatever that leads me to say and to whom. I am here to serve the higher purpose of being that is me.

Do I have it all figured out? That question demonstrates that part of me still claims something separate. When I am truly at one with the divine, the human questions will no longer come up as my questions. I will only know good and allness. I will know only Love and be love.

Isn't that why we're all here in the end? To choose to be the fullest expression of who we are, the divine likeness, the image of Love?

Choose to be you. Choose to be the real you based on Spirit. Choose possibilities not problems. Choose love not fear. Choose good not evil. Choose truth not error. Choose life not death. Choose to create not complain. Choose limitless not limited. Choose victor not victim. Choose release not attachment. Choose flow not struggle. Choose abundance not lack. Choose health not sickness. Choose progress not stagnation. Choose infinite not finite. Choose miracles not misery. Choose playing not winning. Choose being not doing. Choose victor not victim, triumph not tragedy. Choose *God's on it* not *Gosh darn it*! Choose to take a stand not take a fall. Choose mission not mess. Choose action not anxiety. Choose reframe not reject. Choose fly not flounder. Choose confirm not confront. Choose clarity not confusion. Choose lesson not less than. Choose direction not distraction. Choose dream not dread. Choose by design not by default. Choose pony not pile. Choose expression not depression. Choose now not then. Choose now here not nowhere. Choose stillness not stress. Choose *for* me not *to* me. Choose all one not alone. Choose give not get. Choose grateful not hateful. Choose Christ not crisis. Choose full not empty. Choose humble and kind and peaceful. Choose to be you. This choice matters.

✳ Conclusion ✳

Choose to live the Up-In-Out way of life. Listen to the still small voice within. Let the Divine guide you to a life of expansion and miracles. It's in Life's best interest for you to follow your calling — to feel completely fulfilled, for your work to align with who you are, for your life to reflect your heart — to be your best self, serve others, and shine. When you shine your brightest, you light the way for others to do the same, and the whole world is lifted up.

To support you in making this choice, I founded *This Choice Matters*. My signature process, **Look Up, Look In, Look Out**, continues to bless clients and anyone who uses this spiritual Swiss Army knife. If you'd like to walk alongside others living the Up-In-Out way, I invite you to join us for any of the programs offered at *This Choice Matters* (thischoicematters.co).

We can all choose to utilize this profound tool, be divinely guided every day, and establish a practice of it.

- **Look Up** — Acknowledge the all-knowing Mind that governs the universe.

- **Look In** — Claim our oneness with this Mind and our ability to hear next steps.

- **Look Out** — Trust our intuition, humbly follow it, and take divinely impelled action.

Each of us here has the opportunity to let divine intuition guide us to the life that's meant for us.

This one choice has changed my life and continues to change my life. It can do the same for you. Now's the time. Choose to Look Up, Look In, Look Out, and be guided to your best possible life. Because your best life doesn't happen by *chance*. It happens by *choice*. This choice matters.

Resources

Visit lookuplookinlookout.com

Feel free to visit our book portal to follow Lisa on social media, download free resources, get information about The Up-In-Out Way Intensive as well as other current programs, workshops, and courses. Sign up for a subscription to daily inspiration and membership in a community of like-minded people from all over the world.

Lisa Taylor is available for select speaking engagements and to support you through scientific prayer. Please contact Lisa at lisataylorcs.com.

Gratitude and Acknowledgements

T hank you to everyone (and everything) who challenged me, sharpened me, and expected more of me; to those who held the vision with me and lifted me higher; to those who paved the way with understanding and expertise in areas where I was a novice; and to those who told me to breathe and return to the place I feared to enter — the cave.

Thank you to the angels who held my hand while I stood alone on the deck during night watch, who lent guidance, permission, and the way forward; to those who stood by me, believed in me, and continued to see and love me despite my lack of availability, truncated conversations, or missteps; and most of all, to those who saw this idea as worthy of publication, knowing the world needs these ideas to transform and uplift lives.

I am grateful beyond words. Thank you, God, for planting this seed and growing it. Whether it bears fruit is in Your hands.

About the Author

Lisa Taylor works for God. For decades, she has lifted her voice — on the airwaves, in boardrooms, in the quiet corners where truth waits to be heard. A news anchor, a storyteller, a teacher. But more than that, a woman who knows one choice can change everything.

An award-winning speaker, author, and spiritual practitioner, she walks with those who are ready — those who will not be bound by the world's small thinking. As Founder of This Choice Matters, she leads seekers to something higher. Not the fleeting applause of man. Not the shifting sands of circumstance. But the firm ground of spiritual law.

She teaches them to listen — not with ears, but with Soul. To be led — not by fear, but by divine intuition. To build a life — not on struggle, but on certainty.

Through her Up-In-Out method, she guides them step-by-step to:

- Look Up — to the source of all wisdom.

- Look In — to the truth of who you are.

- Look Out — and move boldly, with God as your compass.

This is not wishful thinking. This is Science.
And the results? Inevitable.
For when you can see who you are, you can be who you are.
Choose to be you. This choice matters.

Lisa lives on an island with her husband and friends — Foxie, Owl, and the heron on the rock. Their two children live in New York and Los Angeles.